LEVEL 2

FRENCH
BEHIND THE WHEEL

An Innovative and Effective Language Program that Ensures Maximum Results with Minimal Effort

SERIES FOUNDED BY MARK FROBOSE

Macmillan Audio

Behind the Wheel French Level 2. Copyright © 2009 by Macmillan Audio. All rights reserved. Previously published in another form by Language Dynamics, copyright © 1982, 2007. All rights reserved. For more information, address Macmillan Audio, 175 Fifth Avenue, New York, NY 10010.

www.macmillanaudio.com

INTRODUCTION

A LETTER FROM THE AUTHOR

Throughout a lifetime of learning and teaching foreign languages, I have always been amazed at how inflexible and difficult most foreign language programs are to use. Most have few or no English equivalents or readily accessible explanations for the student to understand what he or she is learning. I used to watch my students scribble notes throughout their books, constantly struggling to grasp and understand concepts. All of that tedium has been eliminated here. In this course you will find English translations for all exercises, written and recorded. As a result, you can focus on learning the language, not searching for answers, and your learning curve in French will be more efficient and more enjoyable.

Bonne Chance! (Good Luck!)

Mark Frobose
Founder, *Behind the Wheel*

ABOUT THIS PROGRAM

Behind the Wheel French 2 is designed to revist the fundamental concepts covered in *Behind the Wheel French 1*—Sentence Building, core vocabulary, key grammar rules—while also expanding and evolving all these areas to give you a broader understanding of the language. French 2 employs short story and dialogue-based lessons to refresh your understanding of French 1 basics in a format that challenges you to take on the next level of functional fluency: reading comprehension and complex sentence construction. And as always, English translations are integrated into every lesson in French 2 so you will never feel like you are completely lost in the material. Additionally, there is a comprehensive reference section at the back of this book which includes vocabulary and common phrases, useful sentence building charts, and grammar reviews and explanations. Together, these two sections give you a chance to interactively practice your French fluency with the benefit of an easily accessible resource for quick reference. The goal, as with all *Behind the Wheel* programs, is to make it as easy as possible for you to succeed at learning a new language.

PRONUNCIATION REVIEW

Vowels

French, like English, has six vowels. They are pronounced as follows:

A *(ah)*
E *(uh)*
I *(ee)*
O *(oh)*
U *(ew)*
Y *(eegreck)*

A   avoir *(ahv wahr)*, appeler *(ah pe lleh)*, attendre *(ah ton druh)*
(to have, to call, to wait)

E   de *(duh)*, deux *(duh)*, ce *(suh)*, le *(luh)*
(of, two, this/that, the)

I   dites *(deet)*, frites *(freet)*, vite *(veet)*
(say, fries, fast)

O   dos *(dough)*, lavabo *(lahv boh)*
(back, sink)

INTRODUCTION v

U   *tu (tew), vu (vew), entendu (on tohn dew)*
(you, seen, heard)

Y   *bicyclette (beeceeclet), J'y vais (jheevay)*
(bicycle, I am going there)

Basic Sounds

ille Pronounced *ee-y-uh*
é   Pronounced like the *ey* of *hey*
è   Pronounced *eh*
h   The *h* in French is always silent
r   Pronounced in the throat and not with the lips
s   Pronounced like an English *z* when single and between vowels; rarely pronounced at the end of a word
gn Sounds similar to *lenient* and *canyon* in English
oe The French *oe* sounds like the *u* in *up* or the *ough* in *enough*

Liaison: The combining of sounds that occurs when a word ending with a consonant is followed by a word starting with a vowel is called a liaison. Here are a few examples of how the French liaison is commonly used.

C'est un homme. (seh tah num)
It's a man.

Les États-Unis (lays ay tahz ew knee)
The United States

Nasal Vowels

When French vowels are followed by an *n* they become nasal and the *n* is pronounced in the nose instead of the mouth.

Accents in French

French has five major accents. Four of these accents typically appear on vowels:

´	*l'accent aigu* (acute accent)	Example: *parlé* (spoken)
`	*l'accent grave* (grave accent)	Example: *très* (very)
^	*l'accent circonflexe* (circumflex accent)	Example: *tôt* (early)
¨	*le tréma* (diaeresis)	Example: *Noël* (Christmas)

The fifth accent is the *cédille* and is used with the consonant *c* before an *a, i,* or *u*. A *cédille* makes the hard *c* sound like a soft *s*.

ç   *la cédille (cedilla)*   Example: *garçon* (boy)

GRAMMAR REVIEW: THE BASICS

The 90% Percent Rule

We will focus on the 90% percent of the time that something is generally true in French. There are, of course, exceptions that will occasionally be mentioned, but we will concentrate on the rule rather than the exceptions. That way you will be right with these simple rules roughly 9 times out of 10. You will learn the exceptions gradually as you become more familiar with the language.

A Noun

A noun is a person, place or thing.

Masculine or Feminine?

In English, all words are neutral, meaning that they are neither masculine nor feminine. In French, though, words are male or female in gender. There are also different ways of saying *a* and *the* that must harmonize with the gender of the nouns. Here are a few examples:

le livre, les livres (the book, the books)

The French word for *book* is *livre* and it is a masculine noun so it uses the article *le* for *the*. If there is more than one book, it is *les livres*, using the plural article *les* for *the* and the plural form of the noun, *livres*. Masculine nouns will also use the article *un* to say *a*. So *a book* is *un livre*.

la maison, les maisons (the house, the houses)

The French word for *house* is *maison* and it is a feminine noun so it uses the article *la* for *the*. If there is more than one house, it is *les maisons*, using the plural article for *the* and the plural form of the noun *house*. Feminine nouns will also use the article *une* to say *a*. So *a house* is *une maison*.

Note: From now on we will abbreviate masculine as (m), feminine as (f), singular as (sing) and plural as (pl).

Formal and Informal

French uses formal and informal ways of speaking to people of different ages, backgrounds, and social standing. *Vous* is *you* in the formal sense while *tu* is a friendly and informal way of saying *you*.

Note: In this text formal will be abbreviated as (form); informal or familiar will be abbreviated as (fam).

Section One

SHORT STORY LESSONS

Each of the following 12 lessons is structured around short stories and dialogues. The vocabulary listing at the start of each lesson will give you a preview of any new or less frequently used vocabulary so that as you read you won't get caught up on unfamiliar terms. Additionally, each story and dialogue is followed by a complete translation in English for quick reference. Each lesson concludes with a Sentence Building Chart featuring vocabulary and grammar elements designed to let you create your own sentences and conversations related to the story or dialogue you have just read. There is a review section for each chart so you can check your progress and test your abilities.

Je Voudrais Lire un Livre (I Want to Read a Book)
J'ai Besoin de Travailler à l'Ordinateur (I Need To Work on the Computer)
Je Suis Désolé(e) Mais J'ai du Retard (I'm Sorry But I'm Behind Schedule)
Beaucoup de Questions (A Lot of Questions)
Mon Anniversaire (My Birthday)
La Gare (The Train Station)
À la Banque (In the Bank)
Pays ou Campagne? (Country or Countryside?)
Combien Coûte l'Autre? (How Much Does the Other Cost?)
Ça N'en Vaut Pas la Peine (It's Not Worth the Trouble)
Quel Temps Fait-Il? (What's The Weather Like?)
Au Restaurant (At a Restaurant)

Je Voudrais Lire un Livre
(I Want to Read a Book)

Vocabulary Preview
d'abord — first of all
ensuite — then/next
plus tard — later
l'exercice — exercise
travailler — to work
obtenir — to get
conduire — to drive
en retard — late

Salut. Je m'appelle Marie. Je veux faire beaucoup de choses aujourd'hui. D'abord, je veux lire un bon livre. J'aime lire. Ensuite, je vais sortir parce qu'il fait beau. Plus tard je vais marcher. Je dois marcher tous les jours parce que j'ai besoin d'exercice. Après, je dois travailler. On doit travailler pour vivre, n'est-ce pas? J'aimerais obtenir un travail avec plus de vacances, mais je ne peux pas maintenant. J'ai besoin de conduire au bureau à dix heures du matin. Je ne veux pas arriver en retard.

Hi. My name is Marie. I want to do a lot of things today. First, I want to read a good book. I like to read. Then, I'm going to go outside because the weather is nice. Later I'm going to walk. I have to walk every day because I need the exercise. Afterwards, I have to work. You have to work in order to live, right? I would like to get a job with more vacation, but I can't now. I need to drive to the office at ten in the morning. I don't want to arrive late.

SHORT STORY LESSONS

Now you try. Use the Sentence Building Chart below to construct your own sentences.

Premièrement (First)	*je voudrais* (I would like)	*faire* (to make)	*un repas* (a meal)
Ensuite (Then)	*je vais* (I'm going to)	*lire* (to read)	*une revue* (a magazine)
Plus tard (Later)	*je dois* (I have to)	*sortir* (to go out)	*avec mes amis* (with my friends)
Après (Afterwards)	*j'ai besoin de* (I need)	*conduire* (to drive)	*ma voiture* (my car)
Finalement (Finally)	*je peux* (I can)	*rester* (to stay)	*mon voyage* (my trip)
		manger (to eat)	*mes vacances* (my vacation)
		se reposer (to relax)	*un peu* (a little)

Let's practice some more. Say the following in French:

1. First I would like to make a meal.
2. Later I'm going to eat a little.
3. Then I can rest.
4. Afterwards I need to go out with my friends.
5. Finally I can relax during my vacation.

Answers: 1. Premièrement je voudrais faire un repas. 2. Plus tard je vais manger un peu. 3. Ensuite je peux rester. 4. Après j'ai besoin de sortir avec mes amis. 5. Finalement je peux me reposer pendant mes vacances.

J'ai Besoin De Travailler sur l'Ordinateur
(I Need To Work on the Computer)

Vocabulary Preview
non plus — neither/not ... either
amusant — fun
tard — late
en plus — in addition
difficile — difficult
facile — easy
au contraire — on the contrary
très — very

Bonjour. Je m'appelle Aline Durand. Je ne veux pas regarder la télé. Je ne vais pas parler au téléphone non plus. Je ne peux pas sortir avec des amis non plus parce qu'il est très tard. En plus, j'ai besoin de travailler sur l'ordinateur. J'aime travailler à l'ordinateur parce que c'est très amusant. Ce n'est pas difficile. Au contraire, c'est très facile.

Good afternoon. My name is Aline Durand. I don't want to watch television. I'm not going to talk on the phone either. I can't go out with friends either because it's very late. Besides, I need to work on the computer. I like to work on the computer because it's a lot of fun. It isn't difficult. On the contrary, it's very easy.

Now you try. Use the Sentence Building Chart below to construct your own sentences.

Je ne veux pas (I don't want)	*regarder la télévision* (to watch television)	*parce que* (because)	*je ne l'aime pas* (I don't like it)
Je ne vais pas (I'm not going to)	*travailler sur l'ordinateur* (to work on the computer)	*d'ailleurs* (besides)	*je ne veux pas le faire* (I don't want to do it)
Ce n'est pas dificile (It isn't difficult)	*sortir avec des amis* (to go out with friends)	*au contraire* (on the contrary)	*c'est très amusant* (it's a lot of fun)
C'est facile (It's easy)	*parler au téléphone* (to talk on the phone)		*j'aime le faire* (I love to do it)

Let's practice some more. Say the following in French:

1. It isn't difficult to work on the computer. On the contrary, it's easy.
2. I don't want to watch television because I don't like it.
3. It's easy to talk on the phone. Besides, I love doing it!
4. I'm not going to go out with friends because I don't want to.
5. It's easy to work on the computer because I love to do it.

Answers: 1. Ce n'est pas dificile de travailler sur l'ordinateur. Au contraire, c'est facile. 2. Je ne veux pas regarder la télévision parce que je ne l'aime pas. 3. C'est facile de parler au telephone. D'ailleurs, j'aime le faire! 4. Je ne vais pas sortir avec des amis parce que je ne veux pas le faire. 5. C'est facile de travailler sur l'ordinateur parce que j'aime le faire.

Je Suis Désolé(e) Mais J'ai du Retard
(I'm Sorry But I'm Behind Schedule)

Vocabulary Preview
avoir du retard — to be behind schedule
le réveil — alarm clock
sonner — to ring
conduire — to drive
le bureau — office
être en retard — to be late
le patron — boss
se fâcher — to get angry
l'ordinateur — computer
donner un coup de fil — to give a (phone) call

Le réveil vient de sonner et je viens de me réveiller. Quelle heure est-il? Mon Dieu. Il est déjà sept heures du matin et je dois conduire une heure et prendre le train encore une heure pour arriver au travail. Où dois-je travailler? Dans un bureau. Je serai en retard. Que puis-je faire? Voyons . . . Je ne sais pas . . . Je peux appeler mon patron et lui dire ce qui s'est passé, mais j'ai peur qu'il se fâche. Je vais travailler à l'ordinateur de toute façon. Je peux peut-être tout faire à la maison. Où est le téléphone? Je lui donne un coup de fil maintenant.

The alarm just rang and I just woke up. What time is it? My goodness. It's already seven in the morning and I have to drive an hour and take the train another hour to get to work. Where do I have to work? In an office. I will be late. What can I do? Let's see...I don't know... I can call my boss on the phone and tell him what happened, but I'm afraid that he's going to get mad. I'm going to work on the computer anyway. Maybe I can do everything at home. Where is the telephone? I'll give him a call right now.

Now you try. Use the Sentence Building Chart below to construct your own sentences. Be sure to use this chart with different clock times to practice your numbers in French.

Il est (it is)	*neuf heures du matin* (nine o'clock in the morning) *trois heures de l'après-midi* (three o'clock in the afternoon) *huit heures du soir* (eight o'clock at night)	*et* (and)	*je suis* (I am) *je serai* (I will be)	*à l'heure* (on time) *en retard* (late) *en avance* (early)

Let's practice some more. Say the following in French:

1. It's eight o'clock in the evening and I'm on time.
2. It's nine o'clock in the morning and I will be late.
3. It's three o'clock in the afternoon and I am early.

Answers: 1. Il est huit heures du soir et je suis à l'heure. 2. Il est neuf heures du matin et je serai en retard. 3. Il est trois heures de l'après-midi et je suis en avance.

Beaucoup de Questions
(A Lot of Questions)

Vocabulary Preview
le livre — book
chez moi — at (my) home
la maison — house
la rue — street
lire — to read
regarder — to watch
parfois — sometimes
cher — expensive

Qu'est-ce que c'est? C'est un livre. C'est quelle sorte de livre? C'est un livre français. Je lis le livre où? Je le lis chez moi. Où est ma maison? Elle est dans une rue. Comment s'appelle la rue? La rue s'appelle "rue des Lilas." Que préférez-vous? Lire des livres ou regarder des films? J'aime les deux. Combien ça coûte d'aller au cinéma? Cela dépend. Parfois jusqu'à 8 euros. C'est très cher. Qui est votre acteur préféré? Combien de livres avez-vous chez vous? Quel livre préférez-vous?

What is this? It's a book. What kind of book is it? It's a French book. Where do I read the book? I read it at home. Where is my house? It's on a street. What's the name of the street? The street is named "rue des Lilas." Which do you like more? Reading books or watching movies? I like both. How much does it cost to go to the movies? It depends. Sometimes up to eight euros. It's very expensive. Who is your favorite actor? How many books do you have in your house? Which book do you like most?

Now you try. Use the Sentence Building Chart below to construct your own sentences.

Qu'est-ce que (What)	il y a (is there/are there)	ici (here)
Lequel (Which)	est (is)	le mien (mine)
Où (Where)	parle (is talking)	le magasin (the store)
Comment (How)	voulez-vous (do you want)	le français (French)
Qui (Who)	préferez-vous (do you prefer)	aller (to go)
Combien (How much/how many)		rester (to stay)
		acheter (to buy)

Let's practice some more. Say the following in French:

1. Where is the store?
2. Who wants to go?
3. How many are there?
4. Which one do you prefer?
5. How many do you want to buy?

Answers: 1. Où est le magasin? 2. Qui veut aller? 3. Combien y a-t-il? 4. Lequel préférez-vous? 5. Combien voulez-vous acheter?

Mon Anniversaire
(My Birthday)

Vocabulary Preview
hier — yesterday
l'après-midi — afternoon
les vêtements — clothes
la fête — party
le soir — the evening
endormi — sleepy
déjeuner — to have lunch
sieste — nap

Salut. Je m'appelle Pierre et vous savez quoi? Aujourd'hui, c'est mon anniversaire. Quel jour sommes-nous? C'est le neuf juillet. Aujourd'hui, j'ai trente-et-un ans. Hier après-midi, je suis allé acheter des vêtements pour ma fête. Hier soir, je suis sorti avec des amis pour célébrer un peu. Ce matin, quand je me suis levé, j'étais un peu endormi parce que je me suis couché tard. Cet après-midi, je prépare la maison pour la fête parce que ce soir je célèbre mon anniversaire. Nous allons danser. Demain matin, ma famille et moi irons déjeuner dans un bon restaurant. Demain après-midi, je vais faire une sieste parce que je serai très fatigué.

Hi. My name is Pierre and do you know what? Today is my birthday. What day is it? It's July ninth. Today I turn thirty-one. Yesterday afternoon I went to buy clothes for my party. Last night I went out with some friends to celebrate a little. This morning I got up a little sleepy because I went to bed late. This afternoon I'm getting the house ready for the party because tonight I'm celebrating my birthday. We're going to dance. Tomorrow morning my family and I are going to have lunch in a good restaurant. Tomorrow afternoon I'm going to take a nap because I will be very tired.

Now you try. Use the Sentence Building Chart below to construct your own sentences.

| *Aujourd'hui* (Today) *Demain* (Tomorrow) *Hier* (Yesterday) | *je vais manger du gateau* (I am going to eat cake) *j'ai dormi toute la journée* (I slept all day) *j'irai au cinéma avec des amis* (I will go to the movies with friends) *je suis content* (I am happy) *j'ai déjeuné dans un bon restaurant* (I had lunch in a good restaurant) *je travaillerai* (I will work) | *parce que* (because) | *c'est mon anniversaire* (it's my birthday) *je dois le faire* (I have to do it) *j'ai dû le faire* (I had to do it) *j'ai voulu le faire* (I wanted to do it) *je voudrais le faire* (I would like to do it) |

Let's practice some more. Say the following in French:

1. Yesterday, I had lunch in a good restaurant because I wanted to.
2. Tomorrow, I will go to the movies with friends because I would like to.
3. Today, I am happy because it's my birthday.
4. Tomorrow, I will work because I have to.
5. Yesterday, I slept all day because I wanted to.

Answers: 1. Hier, j'ai déjeuné dans un bon restaurant parce que j'ai voulu le faire. 2. Demain, j'irai au cinéma parce que je voudrais le faire. 3. Aujourd'hui, je suis content parce que c'est mon anniversaire. 4. Demain, je travaillerai parce que je dois le faire. 5. Hier, j'ai dormi toute la journée parce que j'ai voulu le faire.

La Gare
(The Train Station)

Vocabulary Preview
derrière — behind
s'inquieter — to be worried
le guide touristique — guide book
l'ambassade américaine — the American embassy
quelqu'un — someone
le chemin — the way/the path

Une dame qui ne connaît pas la gare demande au contrôleur s'il sait quel train elle doit prendre et à quelle heure il part.

Dame: *Savez-vous quel train va à Paris?*
Contrôleur: *Oui je le sais. Celui qui est derrière vous part pour Paris à huit heures du soir. Vous connaissez Paris?*
Dame: *Je ne connais pas mais je vais connaître.*
Contrôleur: *Vous savez quoi? Paris est une ville grande et belle. Mais il faut savoir où aller pour vraiment bien la connaître.*
Dame: *Je ne m'inquiète pas pour ça. J'ai un guide touristique. Mais je veux savoir où se trouve l'ambassade américaine.*
Contrôleur: *Je ne la connais pas. Mais je peux demander si vous voulez.*
Dame: *Non merci. Je vais demander à quelqu'un dans le train qui va à Paris et qui connaît le chemin. Merci quand même.*

A lady who isn't familiar with the train station asks the conductor if he knows which train she should take and what time it leaves.

Lady: Do you know which train is going to Paris?
Conductor: Yes, I know. This one that is behind you leaves for Paris at eight p.m. Do you know Paris?

Lady:	I'm not familiar with it but I'm going to be.
Conductor:	Do you know what? Paris is a big and beautiful city. But you have to know where to go in order to really know it well.
Lady:	I'm not worried about that. I have a guide book. But I do want to know where the American embassy is located.
Conductor:	I'm not familiar with it. But I can ask if you want.
Lady:	No thanks. I'm going to ask someone on the train who is going to Paris and who knows the way. Thanks anyway.

Now you try. Use the Sentence Building Chart below to construct your own sentences.

Il est très important (It is very important) *On doit* (One has to)	*savoir où aller* (knowing where to go) *savoir où manger* (knowing where to eat) *savoir comment parler la langue* (knowing how to speak the language) *connaître la ville* (knowing the city) *payer d'avance* (pay in advance)

Let's practice some more. Say the following in French:

1. One has to know how to speak the language.
2. It is very important to know where to go.
3. You've got to pay in advance.
4. It is very important to know how.
5. Knowing where to eat doesn't worry me.

Answers: 1. On doit savoir comment parler la langue. 2. Il est très important de savoir où aller. 3. Tu dois payer d'avance. 4. Il est très important de savoir comment faire. 5. Savoir où manger ne m'inquiète pas.

A la Banque
(At the Bank)

Vocabulary Preview
bien sûr — of course/certainly
des chèques de voyage — traveler's checks
à l'étranger — abroad
n'importe où — anywhere/no matter where
le taux de change — the exchange rate
le guichetier — counterperson/teller

Dame: *Bonjour. Pourriez-vous encaisser ce chèque pour moi s'il vous plaît?*
Guichetier: *Bien sûr Madame. Je peux tout vous donner en liquide si vous avez un compte chez nous.*
Dame: *Oui, j'ai un compte chez vous. J'aimerais aussi des chèques de voyage. Ils les encaisseront à l'étranger?*
Guichetier: *Bien sûr Madame. Vous allez pouvoir les encaisser n'importe où à l'étranger. Dans quels pays allez-vous?*
Dame: *Je suis allée aux États-Unis l'année dernière. Cette année je vais au Mexique.*
Guichetier: *C'est bien! Vous pouvez encaisser ces chèques de voyage en pesos, euros, dollars, peu importe. La seule chose que vous devez d'abord faire c'est les signer.*
Dame: *Maintenant je comprends, avec la signature ils les encaissent pour moi. Vous savez le taux de change des euros en pesos?*
Guichetier: *Je ne sais pas mais je peux vous le dire dans une seconde. Excusez-moi (le guichetier s'en va pour demander.)*

Lady: Hello. Can you cash this check for me please?
Teller: Certainly, ma'am. I can give you everything in cash if you have an account with us.

Lady: Yes, I have an account with you. I would like to get some traveler's checks, too. Will they cash them for me abroad?
Teller: Of course, ma'am. You're going to be able to cash them anywhere abroad. Which countries are you going to?
Lady: I went to the United States last year. This year I'm going to Mexico.
Teller: How nice! You can cash these traveler's checks into pesos, euros, dollars, whatever. The only thing you have to do first is sign them.
Lady: Now I understand, with the signature they'll cash them for me. Do you know the exchange rate from euros to pesos?
Teller: I don't know but I can tell you in a second. Excuse me (the teller goes out to ask.)

Now you try. Use the Sentence Building Chart below to construct your own sentences.

Pourriez-vous (Could you?)	*me donner tout en liquide* (give me everything in cash) *m'aider avec ceci* (help me with this) *encaisser ce chèque pour moi* (cash this check for me)

Let's practice some more. Say the following in French:

1. Could you give me everything in cash please?
2. Could you cash this check for me please?
3. Could you help me with this please?

Answers: 1. Pourriez-vous me donner tout en liquide s'il vous plaît? 2. Pourriez-vous encaisser ce chèque pour moi s'il vous plaît? 3. Pourriez-vous m'aider avec ceci s'il vous plaît?

Pays ou Campagne?
(Country or Countryside?)

Vocabulary Preview
plusieurs — several
les bâtiments — buildings
les arbes — trees
les rivièrs — rivers
les lacs — lakes
les forêts — forests
les montagnes — mountains
les magasins — stores

Il y a beaucoup de pays dans le monde. En Europe il y en a plusieurs. Il y a la France, l'Italie, l'Espagne, l'Allemagne, et beaucoup d'autres. Les États-Unis sont un pays aussi, n'est-ce pas? Oui, bien sûr. Et tous les pays ont des villes et des campagnes. Q'y a-t-il dans les villes? Il y a des bâtiments, des rues, des musées, des bureaux, et beaucoup de monde. Dans les campagnes, il y a quoi? Il y a des arbres, des rivières, des lacs, des forêts, et des montagnes. Une chose qui n'existe pas dans les campagnes, ce sont les magasins. Vous devez faire vos courses en ville, pas à la campagne.

There are many countries in the world. In Europe there are several. There is France, Italy, Spain, Germany and many, many others. The United States is a country too, isn't it? Yes, of course. And all countries have cities and countrysides. What's in the cities? There are buildings, streets, museums, offices, and a whole lot of people. What's in the country? There are trees, rivers, lakes, woods, and mountains. One thing there isn't in the country are stores. You have to do your shopping in the city, not in the country.

Now you try. Use the Sentence Building Chart below to construct your own sentences.

Il y a (There is/there are)	*rues* (streets)	*dans le monde* (in the world)
Il y aura (There is going to be)	*musées* (museums)	*dans la ville* (in the city)
Je vois (I see)	*arbres* (trees)	*à la fête* (at the party)
Tu vas voir (You're going to see)	*rivières* (rivers)	*dans le parc* (in the park)
J'ai visité (I visited)	*lacs* (lakes)	*a l'ouest* (to the West)
	forêts (forests)	*dans les montagnes* (in the mountains)

Let's practice some more. Say the following in French:

1. There are going to be a lot of people at the party.
2. You are going to see trees in the park.
3. There are museums in the city.
4. I visited a lot of countries in the world.
5. I see forests in the mountains.

Answers: 1. Il y aura beaucoup de monde à la fête. 2. Tu vas voir beaucoup d'arbres dans le parc. 3. Il y a des musées dans la ville. 4. J'ai visité beaucoup de pays dans le monde. 5. Je vois des forêts dans les montagnes.

Combien Coûte l'Autre?
(How Much Does the Other Cost?)

Vocabulary Preview
la vendeuse — saleswoman
le magasin — the store
les vêtements — clothes
montrer — to show
parfois — sometimes
dur — hard/difficult

Combien de personnes il y a dans le magasin? Il y en a deux. Ce sont des hommes ou des femmes? Les deux sont des femmes. Une est une vendeuse qui travaille dans le magasin de vêtements et l'autre est sa cliente. Que font-elles? La vendeuse montre plusieurs robes à la cliente. La cliente essaye de décider laquelle elle veut. Elle demande les prix. La cliente dit, "Combien coûte celle-ci et combien coûte l'autre?" Parfois c'est très dur de choisir!

How many people are in the store? There are two. Are they men or women? Both are women. One is a saleslady that works in the clothing store and the other is her customer. What are they doing? The saleslady is showing several dresses to the customer. The customer is trying to decide which one she wants. She is asking for prices. The customer says, "How much is this one and how much does the other cost?" Sometimes it's very hard to choose!

Now you try. Use the Sentence Building Chart below to construct your own sentences.

Qui (Who)	*vous montre* (is showing you)	*comment on le dit* (how it is said)
Je (I)	*lui donne* (is giving him/her)	*combien ça coûte* (how much it costs)
Elle (She)	*lui dit* (is telling him/her)	*quelle est la taille* (what size it is)
La vendeuse (The saleswoman)	*lui demande* (is asking him/her)	*ma carte de crédit* (my credit card)

Let's practice some more. Say the following in French:

1. The saleswoman is showing me the pants.
2. I'm asking her what size it is.
3. She is asking me something.
4. I am giving her my credit card.
5. She is showing me a dress.

Answers: 1. La vendeuse me montre les pantalons. 2. Je lui demande quelle est la taille. 3. Elle me demande quelque chose. 4. Je lui donne ma carte de crédit. 5. Elle me montre une robe.

Ça N'en Vaut Pas la Peine
(It's Not Worth the Trouble)

Vocabulary Preview
au lieu de — instead of
se peigner — to comb one's hair
se maquiller — to apply make-up
s'habiller — to get dressed
les chaussures — shoes
acheter — to buy

Parfois je pense que ça ne vaut pas la peine de se préparer. Au lieu de passer autant de temps à me peigner, à me maquiller, à m'habiller et à mettre des chaussures, je pourrais faire des choses plus importantes. Quoi par exemple? Aller faire les courses et acheter plus de vêtements, bien sûr!

Sometimes I think that it's not worth the trouble getting ready. Instead of spending so much time combing my hair, putting on make-up, getting dressed and trying on shoes, I could be doing more important things. Like what for example? Going shopping to buy more clothes, of course!

SHORT STORY LESSONS

Now you try. Use the Sentence Building Chart below to construct your own sentences.

Je me peigne (I am combing my hair) *Je m'habille* (I am getting dressed) *Je me maquille* (I am putting on make-up) *Je parle au téléphone* (I am talking on the phone) *Je mets mes chaussures* (I am putting on my shoes)	*c'est pourquoi* (that's why) *donc* (therefore)	*je ne peux pas aller* (I can't go) *je suis occupé(e)* (I'm busy) *je suis en retard* (I'm behind schedule) *je ne suis pas prêt(e)* (I'm not ready) *je prends assez de temps* (I'm spending so much time)

Let's practice some more. Say the following in French:

1. I'm combing my hair. That's why I'm taking so long.
2. I'm getting dressed. Therefore I can't go.
3. I'm talking on the phone. That's why I'm behind schedule.
4. I'm putting on make-up. That's why I'm busy.
5. I'm putting on shoes. Therefore I'm not ready.

Answers: 1. Je me peigne. C'est pourquoi je prends assez de temps. 2. Je m'habille. Donc je ne peux pas aller. 3. Je parle au téléphone. C'est pourquoi je suis en retard. 4. Je me maquille. C'est pourquoi je suis occupé(e). 5. Je mets mes chassures. Donc je ne suis pas prêt(e).

Quel Temps Fait-Il?
(What's The Weather Like?)

Vocabulary Preview
le climat — climate
déménager — to move
les nuages — clouds
le ciel — sky
la valise — suitcase
l'imperméable — raincoat
le parapluie — umbrella
le manteau — coat
dessous — below
la prochaine — next

Anne a vécu dans quatre villes différentes avec quatre climats distincts en moins d'un an. Où est-elle allée? Eh bien, d'abord elle a déménagé à Phoenix. Quel temps faisait-il là-bas? Il y avait beaucoup de soleil, c'était sec, et il faisait chaud tous les jours. Il n'y avait presque pas de nuages dans le ciel et il ne pleuvait presque jamais. Même si Anne aimait beaucoup Phoenix, ils l'ont muté à Chicago à l'automne. A Chicago, il y avait toujours du vent, c'était humide en été et il faisait beaucoup plus froid en hiver. Dès que la pauvre Anne avait défait ses valises, elle devait à nouveau les refaire parce que son patron l'a appelé pour l'informer qu'ils allaient la muter. Encore? Où cette fois-ci? À Seattle! Quel temps fait-il là-bas? Il pleut constamment. Ce qui est bien c'est qu'Anne a un imperméable et un bon parapluie. Le dernier déménagement d'Anne était à Minneapolis et bien qu'elle porte un manteau, un bonnet, une écharpe, elle y tremble encore de froid. Il neige huit mois de l'année et la température descend souvent en dessous de zéro. Normalement où que l'on aille, il fait chaud en été, il y a du vent en automne, il pleut et il fait frais au printemps et il neige et il fait froid en hiver. Anne a vécu dans des conditions climatiques extrêmes partout où elle a déménagé. Où Anne va-t-elle maintenant? Quelle est sa prochaine destination? Anne est fatiguée de déménager et elle cherche un autre travail où ils ne la muteront plus jamais. Anne est fatiguée de déménager!

Anne has lived in four different cities with four distinct climates in less than a year. Where did she go? Well, first she moved to Phoenix. What was the weather like there? There was a lot of sun, it was dry, and it was hot every day. There were hardly any clouds in the sky and it almost never rained. As much as Anne liked Phoenix, they transferred her to Chicago in the fall. In Chicago it was always windy, it was humid in the summer, and it was much colder in the winter. As soon as poor Anne had unpacked her suitcases she had to pack them again because her boss called her to inform her that they were going to transfer her. Again? Where to this time? To Seattle! What's the weather like there? It rains constantly. The good thing is that Anne has a raincoat and a good umbrella. Anne's last move was to Minneapolis and in spite of the fact that she's wearing a coat, a hat, and a scarf she is still shivering from cold over there. It snows eight months out of the year and the temperature often goes down below zero. Normally, wherever you go, it's hot in the summer, it's windy in the fall, it rains and it's cool in the spring and it snows and is cold in the winter. Anne has lived in extreme climate conditions everywhere she has moved. Where is Anne going now? What is her next destination? Anne has gotten tired of moving and is looking for another job where they never ever transfer her again. Anne is tired of moving!

Now you try. Use the Sentence Building Chart below to construct your own sentences.

J'avais habité (I have lived)	*à Madrid* (in Madrid)	*pendant* (for)	*un an* (a year)
J'ai habité (I lived)	*à Londres* (in London)		*cinq ans* (five years)
J'ai seulement visité (I only visited)	*à Paris* (in Paris)		*un mois* (a month)
	au Mexique (in Mexico)		*trois jours* (three days)
			quelques heures (a few hours)
			toute ma vie (my whole life)

Let's practice some more. Say the following in French:

1. I have lived in Paris.
2. I lived in Barcelona for a year.
3. I only visited Mexico for three days.
4. I lived in Madrid for a month.
5. I only visited London for a few hours.

Answers: 1. J'avais habité à Paris. 2. J'ai habité a Barcelone pendant un an. 3. J'ai seulement visité Mexique pendant trois jours. 4. J'ai habité à Madrid pendant un mois. 5. J'ai seulement visité Londres pendant quelques heures.

Au Restaurant
(At a Restaurant)

Vocabulary Preview

le faim — hunger
la soif — thirst
la pomme de terre — potato
le légume — vegetable
le poisson — fish
le poulet — chicken
une salade verte — green salad
la serviette — napkin

Charles: *J'ai très faim. Je meurs de faim. J'ai soif aussi.*
Angèle: *Serveur, le menu s'il vous plaît.*
Serveur: *Bien sûr, Madame. Voici le menu. Que désirez-vous commander?*
Charles: *J'ai envie d'un filet mignon avec des pommes de terre et des légumes. C'est servi avec du pain? Blanc ou complet?*
Serveur: *Comme vous désirez.*
Charles: *Complet, s'il vous plaît.*
Angèle: *Le poisson et le poulet me plaisent bien. Ce soir, j'aurai le poisson. Avec une salade verte, s'il vous plaît.*
Serveur: *Et comme boissons?*
Charles: *Du vin rouge pour moi et un verre de vin blanc pour ma femme, s'il vous plaît.*
Serveur: *Bien sûr. Autre chose?*
Angèle: *Oui. Soyez bien aimable de nous apporter deux serviettes et de l'eau s'il vous plaît. Et j'aimerais un café avec le dessert.*
Serveur: *Tout de suite, Madame.*

Charles: I'm really hungry. I'm dying of hunger. I'm thirsty, too.
Angela: Waiter, the menu please.

Waiter: Sure, ma'am. Here's the menu. What do you wish to order?
Charles: I feel like a filet mignon with potatoes and vegetables. Does it come with bread? White or wheat?
Waiter: Whatever you want.
Charles: Wheat, please.
Angela: The fish and the chicken appeal to me. Tonight, I'll have the fish. With a green salad, please.
Waiter: And to drink?
Charles: Red wine for me and a glass of white wine for my wife, please.
Waiter: Of course. Anything else?
Angela: Yes. Be kind enough to bring us two napkins and more water, please. And I would like coffee with the dessert.
Waiter: Right away, ma'am.

Now you try. Use the Sentence Building Chart below to construct your own sentences.

Auriez-vous l'amabilité de (Would you be kind enough to)	*nous apporter plus de café* (bring us more coffee)
	me dire combien ça coûte (tell me how much it costs)
	me donner l'addition (give me the bill)
	me dire où sont les toilettes (tell me where the bathroom is)
	m'aider (help me)

Let's practice some more. Say the following in French:

1. Would you be kind enough to bring us more coffee, please.
2. Would you be kind enough to give me the bill, please.
3. Would you be kind enough to help me, please.
4. Would you be kind enough to tell me where the bathroom is, please.
5. Would you be kind enough to tell me how much it costs, please.

Answers: 1. Auriez-vous l'amabilité de nous apporter plus de café, s'il vous plaît. 2. Auriez-vous l'amabilité de me donner l'addition, s'il vous plaît. 3. Auriez-vous l'amabilité de m'aider, s'il vous plaît. 4. Auriez-vous l'amabilité de me dire où sont les toilettes, s'il vous plaît. 5. Auriez-vous l'amabilité de me dire combien ça coûte, s'il vous plaît.

Section Two

REFERENCE

This section includes vocabulary and common phrases lists, Sentence Building Charts, and grammar explanations. It is designed to be a quick reference for you as you are doing the lessons in this book, and also as you begin putting your French into practice in real life.

Vocabulary

Common Phrases and Useful Expressions

Sentence Building Charts

Grammar

VOCABULARY

Time

aujourd'hui — today
ce soir — tonight
demain — tomorrow
hier — yesterday
le matin — morning
hier matin — yesterday morning
ce matin — this morning
demain matin — tomorrow morning
l'après-midi — afternoon
hier après-midi — yesterday afternoon
cet après-midi — this afternoon
demain après-midi — tomorrow afternoon
le soir — evening/night
hier soir — last night
ce soir — tonight
demain soir — tomorrow night
la semaine — week
le mois — month
le mois dernier — last month
ce mois — this month
le mois prochain — next month
l'an — the year
l'année dernière — last year
cette année — this year
l'année prochaine — next year
à l'heure — on time
en retard — late
en avance — early
plus tard — later
maintenant — now
quelquefois — sometimes

souvent — often
bientôt — soon
la première fois — the first time
la prochaine fois — the next time
la dernière fois — the last time
la seule fois — the only time
toute la journée — all day
toute la nuit — all night
tout à coup — suddenly
midi — noon
minuit — midnight
du matin (dix heures du matin) — in the morning (clock time, as in 10 a.m.)
de l'après-midi (quatre heures de l'après-midi) — in the afternoon (clock time, as in 4 p.m.)
du soir (huit heures du soir) — at night (clock time, as in 8 p.m.)
et quart — quarter past
et demie — half past
moins le quart — quarter to

Money

en liquide — in cash
un chèque — check
un cart de crédit — credit card
le taux de change — exchange rate
de dollars en euros — from dollars to euros
dépenser de l'argent — to spend money

Numbers

un — one
deux — two
trois — three
quatre — four
cinq — five

six — six
sept — seven
huit — eight
neuf — nine
dix — ten
onze — eleven
douze — twelve
treize — thirteen
quatorze — fourteen
quinz — fifteen
seize — sixteen
dix-sept — seventeen
dix-huit — eighteen
dix-neuf — nineteen
vingt — twenty
vingt-deux — twenty-two
trente — thirty
trente-trois — thirty-three
quarante — forty
quarante-quatre — forty-four
cinquante — fifty
cinquante-cinq — fifty-five
soixante — sixty
soixante-six — sixty-six
soixante-dix — seventy
soixante-dix-sept — seventy-seven
quatre-vingt — eighty
quatre-vingt-huit — eighty-eight
quatre-vingt-dix — ninety
quatre-vingt-dix-neuf — ninety-nine
cent — one hundred
cinq cents — five hundred
sept cents — seven hundred

neuf cents — nine hundred
mille — one thousand

Travel
par avion — by plane
en voiture — by car
par train — by train
le billet — ticket
à l'étranger — abroad
un souvenir — souvenir/memory
en vacances — on vacation
l'ambassade — embassy
le pays — country
la campagne — countryside
la langue — language
la nationalité — nationality
les États-Unis — the United States
la France — France
la Suisse — Switzerland
la Belgique — Belgium

Food and Restaurant
le serveur/la serveuse — waiter/waitress
la carte — menu
l'addition — check
le petit déjeuner — breakfast
le déjeuner — lunch
le dîner — dinner
la fourchette — fork
le couteau — knife
la cuillère — spoon
la serviette — napkin
la tasse — cup

le verre — glass
les glaçons — ice cubes
le pain — bread
le buerre — butter
la confiture — jam
le sel — salt
le poivre — pepper
les oeufs — eggs
la soupe — soup
la salade — salad
le poulet — chicken
le steak — steak
le poisson — fish
les moules — mussels
les fruits de mer — seafood
la viande — meat
les légumes — vegetables
les pâtes — pasta
les pommes de terre — potatoes
les pommes frites — french fries
le porc — pork
le dessert — dessert
le gâteau — cake
les biscuits — cookies
la glace — ice cream
le fromage — cheese
le jambon — ham
la bière — beer
le vin rouge — red wine
le vin blanc — white wine
le jus — juice
le jus d'orange — orange juice
la limonade — lemon soda
le lait — milk

le café — coffee
la crème — cream
le sucre — sugar

Descriptions
rouge — red
jaune — yellow
orange — orange
bleu(e) — blue
blanc(he) — white
marron — brown
noir(e) — black
vert(e) — green
grand(e) — big/tall
petit(e) — small/short(person)
long(ue) — long
court(e) — short (length)
large — wide
étroit(e) — narrow
épais(se) — thick
gros(se) — fat
mince — thin

Family
ma famille — my family
la femme — woman/wife
le mari — husband
les époux — spouses
les parents — parents
la mère — mother
le père — father
les enfants — children
le fils — son
la fille — girl/daughter

les grands-parents — grandparents
les petits-enfants — grand children
la belle-mère — mother-in-law
le beau-père — father-in-law
le beau-fils — son-in-law
la belle-fille — daughter-in-law
la tante — aunt
l'oncle — uncle
le cousin — male cousin
la cousine — female cousin
le neveu — nephew
la nièce — niece

Question Words
combien — how much
quoi — what
lequel/laquelle — which
où — where
comment — how
qui — who
pourquoi — why
quand — when
de qui — whose

Commands
vas-y! allez-y! — go!
écoute! écoutez! — listen!
viens! venez! — come!
attends! attendez! — wait!
allumez! — turn on!
éteignez! — turn off!

COMMON PHRASES AND USEFUL EXPRESSIONS

General Phrases
Enchanté(e) — It's nice to meet you
Merci beaucoup — Thank you very much
De rien — You're welcome
Il n y a pas de quoi — It was no trouble
Je vous en prie — It was my pleasure
Auriez-vous l'amabilité de — Would you be kind enough to
Pardon — Excuse me
Répétez s'il vous plaît — Repeat, please
Je suis désolé(e) — I'm sorry
Je ne comprends pas — I don't understand
Je ne sais pas — I don't know
Je ne peux pas — I can't
J'ai besoin de — I need
Je veux dire — I mean
D'accord — Alright
Tout de suite — Right away
J'arrive — I'm coming
Voilà — Here it is
Bien sûr — Of course
A bientôt — See you soon
A vos souhaits — Bless you (after a sneeze)
Ce n'est pas possible — It's not possible
C'est interdit — It's forbidden

Directions
Où est-ce? — Where is it?
C'est a quelle distance? — How far is it?
Où dois-je descendre? — Where should I get off?
C'est près ou loin? — Is it near or far?
Tournez à droite — Turn right

Tournez à gauche — Turn left
Allez tout droit — Go straight on

Weather

Quel temps fait-il? — What's the weather like?
Il fait beau — The weather is nice
Il fait mauvais — The weather is bad
Il fait chaud — It's hot
Il fait froid — It's cold
Il fait frais — It's cool
Il pleut — It's raining
Il fait du soleil — It's sunny
Il neige — It's snowing
Il est nuageux — It's cloudy
Le ciel est clair — It's clear (cloudless)
Il fait du vent — It's windy

Common Questions

Qu'est-ce que c'est? — What is this/that?
Qui est-ce? — Who is it?
Pourquoi? — Why?
De quel genre? — What kind?
De quelle taille? — What size?
De quelle couleur? — What color?
Il y a combien? — How many are there?
Comment dit-on en français? — How do you say in French?
Qu'est-ce que ça veut dire? — What does this mean?
Qu'est-ce que je dois faire? — What should I do?
Qu'est-ce qu'on parle? — What is spoken?
Ça vaut combien? — What's it worth?
Ça coûte combien? — How much does it cost?
Pourriez-vous me recommander quelquechose? — Can you recommend something?
Pourriez-vous me dire? — Can you tell me?

Où sont les toilettes? — Where is the bathroom?
Comment vous appelez-vous? — What's your name?
Quel âge avez-vous? — How old are you?
Comment allez-vous? — How are you?
Quoi de neuf? — What's new?

Idiomatic Expressions

Ça n'en vaut pas la peine — It's not worth it
À quelque chose malheur est bon — Every cloud has a silver lining
Ce qui vient de la flûte s'en va par le tambour — Easy come, easy go
L'avenir appartient à ceux qui se lèvent tôt — God helps the early riser
Mieux vaut un que deux tu l'auras — A bird in the hand is worth two in the bush
On ne rattrape pas le temps perdu — Lost time is not found again
Un chien qui aboie ne mord pas — A barking dog doesn't bite
Qu'est-ce qui vous plairait? — What looks good to you?
Je meurs de faim — I'm dying of hunger
Faites comme chez vous — Make yourself at home
C'est plus facile à dire qu'à faire — Easier said than done
C'est la vie — That's life
Il n'y a pas de fumée sans feu — Where there's smoke, there's fire
On ne fait pas d'omelette sans casser des oeufs — You can't make an omlette without breaking a few eggs
Quand on veut, on peut — Where there's a will, there's a way
Le temps, c'est de l'argent — Time is money
Donne-moi un coup de main — Give me a hand
Un coup de chance — A piece of luck
Casse-toi! — Get out of here
Ça ne casse rien — It's no big deal
A votre bon coeur! — Thank you kindly!
Tant pis — Too bad
Tant mieux pour toi — Good for you
On est toujours mieux chez soi — Home sweet home

SENTENCE BUILDING CHARTS

The following Sentence Building Charts cover basic grammar and vocabulary, providing a quick and easy-to-use reference. Combine elements across the columns to create your own original sentences.

Sentence Building: First Person Present Tense

Je veux (I want)	*parler* (to talk/speak)	*danser* (to dance)	*au téléphone* (on the telephone)	*à l'étranger* (abroad)
J'aime (I like)	*obtenir* (to get)	*travailler* (to work)	*avec des amis* (with friends)	*un souvenir* (a souvenir)
Je peux (I can)	*dormir* (to sleep)	*aller* (to go)	*tout* (everything)	*tout de suite* (right away)
Je dois (I have to)	*voyager* (to travel)	*nager* (to swim)	*bonne nourriture* (good food)	*maintenant* (now)
On doit (One has to)	*sortir* (to go out)	*faire* (to do/make)	*beaucoup de choses* (a lot of things)	*quelque chose* (something)
Je voudrais (I would like)	*donner* (to give)	*voir* (to see)	*une lettre* (a letter)	*au travail* (to work)
J'ai besoin de (I need)	*manger* (to eat)	*écrire* (to write)	*un chèque* (a check)	*au centre-ville* (downtown)
	marcher (to walk)	*apprendre* (to learn)	*le français* (French)	*dans l'hôtel* (in the hotel)
				du magasin (from the store)

Note: Remember, you can easily make any of these sentences negative by adding *ne* before the verb and *pas* after the verb, for example, *je ne veux pas* means *I don't want*.

Sentence Building: Compound Sentences
MAIS (BUT)

Je voudrais (I would like)	*travailler* (to work)	*mais* (but)	*je ne peux pas* (I can't)
Je vais (I'm going to)	*marcher* (to walk)		*ça ne fait rien* (it doesn't matter)
Je dois (I have to)	*payer* (to pay)		*ce n'est pas possible* (it isn't possible)
J'ai besoin de (I need to)	*essayer* (to try)		*je n'ai pas envie de le faire* (I don't feel like it)
Je préfère (I prefer)	*nager* (to swim)		*c'est interdit* (it's forbidden)
	manger (to eat)		*je n'ai pas d'argent* (I don't have money)
	aller (to go)		*il fait trop chaud* (it's too hot)
	continuer (to continue)		*il fait trop froid* (it's too cold)
	arrêter (to stop)		*c'est trop tard* (it's too late)

PARCE QUE (BECAUSE)

Je ne veux pas (I don't want)	*travailler* (to work)	*parce que* (because)	*je ne peux pas* (I can't)
Je ne vais pas (I'm not going)	*marcher* (to walk)		*je n'ai pas le temps* (I don't have time)
Je ne dois pas (I don't have to)	*payer* (to pay)		*ce n'est pas possible* (it isn't possible)
Je n'ai pas besoin de (I don't need)	*essayer* (to try)		*je n'ai pas envie de le faire* (I don't feel like it)
Je préfère de ne pas (I prefer not)	*nager* (to swim)		*c'est interdit* (it's forbidden)
	manger (to eat)		*je n'ai pas d'argent* (I don't have money)
	aller (to go)		*il fait trop chaud* (it's too hot)
	continuer (to continue)		*il fait trop froid* (it's too cold)
	arrêter (to stop)		*c'est trop tard* (it's too late)

Sentence Building: More Practice Using the Negative

Je ne veux pas (I don't want)	*deviner* (to guess)	*la réponse* (the answer)
Je ne peux pas (I can't)	*dormir* (to sleep)	*tard* (late)
Je n'aime pas (I don't like)	*obtenir* (to get)	*la nuit* (at night)
Je ne dois pas (I don't have to)	*sortir* (to go out/leave)	*toute la journée* (all day)
Vous n'aimez pas (You don't like)	*travailler* (to work)	*la raison* (the reason)
Vous ne devez pas (You don't have to)	*manger* (to eat)	*tout le monde* (everyone)
	faire (to do/make)	*quelque chose de bon* (something good)
	laisser (to leave)	*rien* (nothing/anything)
	envoyer (to send)	*un message* (a message)
	voir (to see)	*ce qui se passe* (what's going on)
	étudier (to study)	*la leçon* (the lesson)
	voyager (to travel)	*en avion* (by plane)
	acheter (to buy)	*les billets* (the tickets)
	vendre (to sell)	*la langue* (the language)
	apprendre (to learn)	*de l'aide* (help)
	demander (to request/order)	*en liquide* (in cash)
	payer (to pay)	*en vacances* (on vacation)
	aller (to go)	*à temps* (on time)
	rentrer (to return)	*le gérant* (the manager)
	demander (to ask)	*un mensonge* (a lie)
	répondre (to answer)	*seule(f)/seul(m)* (alone)
	trouver (to find out)	*la vérité* (the truth)
	marcher (to walk)	
	dire (to say/tell)	

Sentence Building: Conjugating être (to be)

Je suis (I am)	*fatigué(e)* (tired)
Tu es (You are)	*malade* (sick)
Il/elle est (He/she/it is)	*heureux/heureuse* (happy)
Nous sommes (We are)	*triste* (sad)
Vous êtes (You are)	*content(e)* (content)
Ils/elles sont (They are)	*ici* (here)
	à la classe (in class)
	près (close)
	loin (far)
	occupé(e) (busy)
	pressé(e) (in a hurry)
	là bas (over there)
	au centre-ville (downtown)

Sentence Building: Conjugating avoir (to have)

Note: In French, you aren't hungry or thirsty, you *have* hunger or thirst. Similarly, you aren't a certain age, you have a certain number of years. French uses the verb *avoir* (to have) for these expressions where English uses the verb *to be*.

J'ai (I have)	*vingt-cinq ans* (25 years of age)
Tu as (You have)	*faim* (hunger)
Il/elle a (He/she has)	*soif* (thirst)
Nous avons (We have)	*froid* (coldness)
Vous avez (You have)	*chaud* (hotness)
Ils ont (They have)	*sommeil* (sleepiness)
	envie de (the desire for/to)
	de la chance (luck)
	besoin de (need)

Sentence Building: Talking about Past Actions

J'ai (I have)	*parlé* (talked/spoken)	*vendu* (to sold)
Tu as (you have)	*dormi* (slept)	*commencé* (started)
Il/elle a (he/she/one has)	*travaillé* (worked)	*terminé* (finished)
Nous avons (we have)	*su* (known)	*commandé* (ordered)
Vous avez (you have)	*connu* (known)	*payé* (paid)
Ils/elles ont (they have)	*mangé* (eaten)	*demandé* (asked)
	fait (done/made)	*répondu* (answered)
	écrit (written)	*conduit* (driven)
	changé (cashed/changed)	*marché* (walked)
	étudié (studied)	*obtenu* (got)
	voyagé (traveled)	*reçu* (received)
	acheté (bought)	

Sentence Building: Talking about Past Action using être

Note: Most verbs in the passé composé are conjugated with *avoir* as in the previous chart. However, some are conjugated with *être*, including all reflexive verbs and verbs such as *aller, venir,* and *mourir* which indicate a change of space or being.

Je suis (I [have])	*entré(e)* (entered)
Tu es (You [have])	*sorti(e)* (gone out)
Il/elle est (He/she [has])	*allé(e)* (gone)
Nous sommes (We [have])	*rentré(e)* (returned)
Vous êtes (You [have])	*parti(e)* (left)
Ils/elles sont (They [have])	

Sentence Building: Talking About Future Actions

Je vais (I am going)	*savoir* (to know/to find out)	*perdre* (to lose)
Tu vas (You are going)	*obtenir* (to get)	*aider* (to help)
Il/elle va (He/she/it is going)	*travailler* (to work)	*laver* (to wash)
Nous allons (We are going)	*aller* (to go)	*trouver* (to find)
Vous allez (You are going)	*manger* (to eat)	*ouvrir* (to open)
Ils/elles vont (They are going)	*sortir* (to go out)	*fermer* (to close)
	commencer (to start)	*chercher* (to look for)
	acheter (to buy)	*raconter* (to tell a story)
	payer (to pay)	*dire* (to say/to tell)
	signer (to sign)	*chanter* (to sing)
	gagner (to win)	*danser* (to danse)

Sentence Building: Objects

Direct and indirect object pronouns take the place of a noun. Some sentences have direct object pronouns, indirect object pronouns, or both. Double object pronouns occur when a sentence has both a direct and an indirect object pronoun. For more information on object pronouns, refer to the grammar section.

Direct Object Pronouns

A direct object receives the action of the verb. You find the direct object by asking the question *what?* or *who?* Direct object pronouns replace the direct objects. There are seven direct object pronouns in French: *me, te, le/l', la/l', nous, vous, les*. In French, the order of the words is reversed so that the direct object comes in the middle of the clause, instead of at the end.

Je veux (I want)	*me* (me)	*aider* (to help)
Vous voulez (you want)	*te* (you)	*vendre* (to sell)
Je vais (I'm going)	*le/l'* (it/him)	*faire* (to do/to make)
Vous allez (you're going)	*la/l'* (it/her)	*acheter* (to buy)
J'ai besoin de (I need)	*nous* (us)	*manger* (to eat)
Vous avez besoin de (you need)	*vous* (you)	*goûter* (to taste)
Je dois (I must)	*les* (them)	*essayer* (to try)
Vous devez (you must)		*donner* (to give)
		payer (to pay)
		parler (to speak)
		dire (to say/to tell)

Indirect Object Pronouns

An indirect object names the person or object to whom or at whom an action is being performed. An indirect object pronoun replaces the indirect object. There are six indirect object pronouns in French. They are: *me, te, lui, nous, vous, leur.*

Je veux (I want)	*me* (me)	*acheter* (to buy)	*un cadeau* (a present)
Vous voulez (You want)	*te* (you)	*donner* (to give)	*la verité* (the truth)
J'ai besoin de (I need)	*lui* (him/her)	*vendre* (to sell)	*l'argent* (the money)
Vous avez besoin de (You need)	*nous* (us)	*louer* (to rent)	*un appartement* (an apartment)
Je dois (I have to)	*vous* (you)	*demander* (to ask for)	*la nouvelle voiture* (the new car)
Vous devez (You have to)	*leur* (them)	*montrer* (to show)	*le secret* (the secret)
			le chemin (the way/the path)

Double Object Pronouns

When you have double object pronouns, some indirect object pronouns (*me, te, se, nous, vous*) come before the direct object pronoun and others (*lui, leur*) come after.

Je (I)	*le lui* (it [m] to/for him)	*donne* (give)
	te le (it [m] to/for you)	*achète* (buy)
	les lui (them to/for him)	*vends* (sell)
	la leur (it [f] to/for them)	*dis* (tell)
	vous la (it [f] to/for you)	*demande* (ask)
		montre (show)
		enseigne (teach)

GRAMMAR

Verb Conjugation Charts

To conjugate a verb is to break it down from the infinitive into its basic forms. First the ending of the verb must be removed to find the stem. Next, certain endings are added to the stem to make the different forms. Understanding the basics of conjugation will allow you to communicate in all subject voices (I, you, he, she, it, they, and we).

Present Tense

Note: The *il/elle* form of the verb can also be used for *it* (*il* or *elle* depending on the gender of *it*) and *on* (*one,* the colletive one as in *one must be prepared*).

PARLER (to talk)
 je parle (I talk)
 tu parles (you talk)
 il/elle parle (he/she talks)
 nous parlons (we talk)
 vous parlez (you talk)
 ils/elles parlent (they talk)

FINIR (to finish)
 je finis (I finish)
 tu finis (you finish)
 il/elle finit (he/she finishes)
 nous finissons (we finish)
 vous finissez (you finish)
 ils/elles finissent (they finish)

RÉPONDRE (to answer)
 je réponds (I answer)
 tu réponds (you answer)

il/elle répond (he/she answers)
nous répondons (we answer)
vous répondez (you answer)
ils/elles répondent (they answer)

MANGER (to eat)
je mange (I eat)
tu manges (you eat)
il/elle mange (he/she eats)
nous mangeons (we eat)
vous mangez (you eat)
ils/elles mangent (they eat)

OUVRIR (to open)
j'ouvre (I open)
tu ouvres (you open)
il/elle ouvre (he/she opens)
nous ouvrons (we open)
vous ouvrez (you open)
ils/elles ouvrent (they open)

FERMER (to close)
je ferme (I close)
tu fermes (you close)
il/elle ferme (he/she closes)
nous fermons (we close)
vous fermez (you close)
ils/elles ferment (they close)

COURIR (to run)
je cours (I run)
tu cours (you run)
il/elle court (he/she runs)
nous courons (we run)

vous courez (you run)
ils/elles courent (they run)

ÉCRIRE (to write)
j'écris (I write)
tu écris (you write)
il/elle écrit (he/she writes)
nous écrivons (we write)
vous écrivez (you write)
ils/elles écrivent (they write)

PRENDRE (to take)
je prends (I take)
tu prends (you take)
il/elle prend (he/she/it takes)
nous prenons (we take)
vous prenez (you take)
ils/elles prennent (they take)

LIRE (to read)
je lis (I read)
tu lis (you read)
il/elle lit (he/she reads)
nous lisons (we read)
vous lisez (you read)
ils/elles lisent (they read)

RECEVOIR (to receive)
je reçois (I receive)
tu reçois (you receive)
il/elle reçoit (he/she receives)
nous recevons (we receive)
vous recevez (you receive)
ils/elles reçoivent (they receive)

ALLER (to go)
je vais (I go)
tu vas (you go)
il/elle va (he/she goes)
nous allons (we go)
vous allez (you go)
ils/elles vont (they go)

SAVOIR (to know facts or information)
je sais (I know)
tu sais (you know)
il/elle sait (he/she knows)
nous savons (we know)
vous savez (you know)
ils/elles savent (they know)

CONNAÎTRE (to know or to be familiar with people, places, or things)
je connais (I know)
tu connais (you know)
il/elle connaît (he/she knows)
nous connaissons (we know)
vous connaissez (you know)
ils/elles conaissent (they know)

The Present Progressive

The progressive tense is used to describe an ongoing action that is occurring at the same time that the statement is written or said. In French, the present and past progressives are formed using *être en train de* (to be in the process of). For the present progressive, you use *être* in the present tense and for the past progressive, you use *être* in the past tense. Examples:

Je suis en train de parler. (I am talking.)
Tu es en train d'écouter. (You are listening.)

Elle est en train d'étudier. (She is studying.)
Nous sommes en train de manger. (We are eating.)

The Passé Composé

The passé composé describes actions that occurred in the past one time and were not repeated. It is formed using either *être* or *avoir* and the past participle of the main verb. Most verbs will use *avoir*. Verbs that indicate motion or a change in physical state typically use *être*, for example *aller* (to go.) All reflexive verbs use *être*.

Verbs that use avoir

PARLER (to talk)
j'ai parlé (I spoke)
tu as parlé (you spoke)
il/elle a parlé (he/she spoke)
nous avons parlé (we spoke)
vous avez parlé (you spoke)
ils ont parlé (they spoke)

FINIR (to finish)
j'ai fini (I finished)
tu as fini (you finished)
il/elle a fini (he/she finished)
nous avons fini (we finished)
vous avez fini (you finished)
ils/elles ont fini (they finished)

RÉPONDRE (to answer)
j'ai répondu (I answered)
tu as répondu (you answered)
il/elle a répondu (he/she answered)
nous avons répondu (we answered)
vous avez répondu (you answered)
ils/elles ont répondu (they answered)

MANGER (to eat)
j'ai mangé (I ate)
tu as mangé (you ate)
il/elle mangé (he/she ate)
nous avons mangé (we ate)
vous avez mangé (you ate)
ils/elles ont mangé (they ate)

OUVRIR (to open)
j'ai ouvert (I opened)
tu as ouvert (you opened)
il/elle a ouvert (he/she opened)
nous avons ouvert (we opened)
vous avez ouvert (you opened)
ils/elles ont ouvert (they opened)

FERMER (to close)
j'ai fermé (I closed)
tu as fermé (you closed)
il/elle a fermé (he/she closed)
nous avons fermé (we closed)
vous avez fermé (you closed)
ils/elles ont fermé (they closed)

COURIR (to run)
j'ai couru (I ran)
tu as couru (you ran)
il/elle a couru (he/she ran)
nous avons couru (we ran)
vous avez couru (you ran)
ils/elles ont couru (they ran)

ÉCRIRE (to write)
j'ai écrit (I wrote)
tu as écrit (you wrote)

il/elle a écrit (he/she wrote)
nous avons écrit (we wrote)
vous avez écrit (you wrote)
ils/elles ont écrit (they wrote)

PRENDRE (to take)
j'ai pris (I took)
tu as pris (you took)
il/elle a pris (he/she took)
nous avons pris (we took)
vous avez pris (you took)
ils/elles ont pris (they took)

LIRE (to read)
j'ai lu (I read)
tu as lu (you read)
il/elle a lu (he/she read)
nous avons lu (we read)
vous avez lu (you read)
ils/elles ont lu (they read)

RECEVOIR (to receive)
j'ai reçu (I received)
tu as reçu (you received)
il/elle a reçu (he/she received)
nous avons reçu (we received)
vous avez reçu (you received)
ils/elles ont reçu (they received)

SAVOIR (to know facts or information)
j'ai su (I knew)
tu as su (you knew)
il/elle a su (he/she knew)
nous avons su (we knew)

vous avez su (you knew)
ils/elles ont su (they knew)

CONNAÎTRE (to know or to be familiar with people, places, or things)
j'ai connu (I knew)
tu as connu (you knew)
il/elle a connu (he/she knew)
nous avons connu (we knew)
vous avez connu (you knew)
ils/elles ont connu (they knew)

Verbs that use être

ALLER (to go)
je suis allé(e) (I went)
tu es allé(e) (you went)
il/elle est allé (he/she went)
nous sommes allé(e)s (we went)
vous êtes allé(es) (you went)
ils/elles sont allé(e)s (they went)

DEVENIR (to become)
je suis devenu(e) (I became)
tu es devenu(e) (you became)
il/elle est devenu(e) (he/she became)
nous sommes devenu(e)s (we became)
vous êtes devenu(e)(s) (you became)
ils/elles sont devenu(s)(es) (they became)

Note: When you use *être* to form the passé composé, the past participle must agree with the subject.

The Imperfect

The imperfect tense is used to describe habitual or continuous past action. For example, *je parlais* (I was talking or I used to talk). Below are examples of how to conjugate regular verbs ending in *-er*, *-ir*, and *-re* in the imperfect tense.

PARLER (to talk/speak)

parl +	ais	*je parlais* (I was talking)
	ais	*tu parlais* (you were talking)
	ait	*il/elle parlait* (he/she was talking)
	ions	*nous parlions* (we were talking)
	iez	*vous parliez* (you were talking)
	aient	*ils/elles parlaient* (they were talking)

SORTIR (to leave)

sort +	ais	*je sortais* (I was leaving)
	ais	*tu sortais* (you were leaving)
	ait	*il/elle sortait* (he/she was leaving)
	ions	*nous sortions* (we were leaving)
	iez	*vous sortiez* (you were leaving)
	aient	*ils/elles sortaient* (they were leaving)

VENDRE (to sell)

vend +	ais	*je vendais* (I was selling)
	ais	*tu vendais* (you were selling)
	ait	*il/elle vendait* (he/she was selling)
	ions	*nous vendions* (we were selling)
	iez	*vous vendiez* (you were selling)
	aient	*ils/elles vendaient* (they were selling)

Many verbs have irregular conjugations in the imperfect. Here a few examples.

CONDUIRE (to drive)
je conduisais (I was driving)
tu conduisais (you were driving)
il/elle conduisait (he/she was driving)
nous conduisions (we were driving)
vous conduisiez (you were driving)
ils/elles conduisaient (they were driving)

FERMER (to close)
je fermerais (I was closing)
tu fermerais (you were closing)
il/elle fermerait (he/she was closing)
nous fermerons (we were closing)
vous fermerez (you were closing)
ils/elles ferment (they were closing)

ÉCRIRE (to write)
j'écrivais (I was writing)
tu écrivais (you were writing)
il/elle écrivait (he/she was writing)
nous écrivions (we were writing)
vous écriviez (you were writing)
ils/elles écrivaient (they were writing)

BOIRE (to drink)
je buvais (I was drinking)
tu buvais (you were drinking)
il/elle buvait (he/she was drinking)
nous buvions (we were drinking)
vous buviez (you were drinking)
ils/elles buvaient (they were drinking)

LIRE (to read)
 je lisais (I was reading)
 tu lisais (you were reading)
 il/elle lisait (he/she was reading)
 nous lisions (we were reading)
 vous lisiez (you were reading)
 ils/elles lisaient (they were reading)

ÉTUDIER (to study)
 j'étudiais (I was studying)
 tu étudiais (you were studying)
 il/elle étudiait (he/she was studying)
 nous étudiions (we were studying)
 vous étudiiez (you were studying)
 ils/elles étudiaient (they were studying)

The Near Future

The Near Future uses the verb *aller* (to go) plus an infinitive.

aller (to go)	Infinitive
je vais (I'm going)	*parler* (to talk/to speak)
tu vas (you are going)	*travailler* (to work)
il/elle va (he/she is going)	*manger* (to eat)
nous allons (we are going)	*sortir* (to go out)
vous allez (you are going)	*essayer* (to try)
ils/elles vont (they are going)	*payer* (to pay)

The Simple Future

The Simple Future is formed by taking the infinitive of a verb and adding specific endings to it as shown here.

Infinitive	*Endings*	*Conjugated Verb Form*
parler	*ai*	*je parlerai* (I will speak)
	as	*tu parleras* (you will speak)

a	*il/elle parlera* (he/she will speak)
ons	*nous parlerons* (we will speak)
ez	*vous parlerez* (you will speak)
ont	*ils/elles parleront* (they will speak)

Note: The above chart refers to regular verbs. Many verbs have irregular stems that do not match the infinitive exactly. For example, the verbs *être*, *avoir*, and *aller* are irregular verbs that must be memorized separately.

ÊTRE (to be)
je serai (I will be)
tu seras (you will be)
il/elle sera (he/she will be)
nous serons (we will be)
vous serez (you will be)
ils/elles seront (they will be)

AVOIR (to have)
j'aurai (I will have)
tu auras (you will have)
il/elle aura (he/she will have)
nous aurons (we will have)
vous aurez (you will have)
ils/elles auront (they will have)

ALLER (to go)
j'irai (I will go)
tu iras (you will go)
il/elle ira (he/she will go)
nous irons (we will go)
vous irez (you will go)
ils/elles iront (they will go)

Here are some more verbs in the simple future.

LIRE (to read)
je lirai (I will read)
tu liras (you will read)
il/elle lira (he/she will read)
nous lirons (we will read)
vous lirez (you will read)
ils/elles liront (they will read)

SAVOIR (to know facts or information)
je saurai (I will know)
tu sauras (you will know)
il/elle saura (he/she will know)
nous saurons (we will know)
vous saurez (you will know)
ils/elles sauront (they will know)

MANGER (to eat)
je mangerai (I will eat)
tu mangeras (you will eat)
il/elle mangera (he/she will eat)
nous mangerons (we will eat)
vous mangerez (you will eat)
ils/elles mangeront (they will eat)

AIMER (to love)
j'aimerai (I will love)
tu aimeras (you will love)
il/elle aimera (he/she will love)
nous aimerons (we will love)
vous aimerez (you will love)
ils/elles aimeront (they will love)

OUVRIR (to open)
j'ouvrirai (I will open)
tu ouvriras (you will open)
il/elle ouvrira (he/she will open)
nous ouvrirons (we will open)
vous ouvrirez (you will open)
ils/elles ouvriront (they will open)

FERMER (to close)
je fermerai (I will close)
tu fermeras (you will close)
il/elle fermera (he/she will close)
nous fermerons (we will close)
vous fermerez (you will close)
ils/elles fermeront (they will close)

VOIR (to see)
je verrai (I will see)
tu verras (you will see)
il/elle verra (he/she will see)
nous verrons (we will see)
vous verrez (you will see)
ils/elles verront (they will see)

ÉTUDIER (to study)
j'étudierai (I will study)
tu étudieras (you will study)
il/elle étudiera (he/she will study)
nous étudierons (we will study)
vous étudierez (you will study)
ils/elles étudieront (they will study)

APPRENDRE (to learn)
j'apprendrai (I will learn)
tu apprendras (you will learn)
il/elle apprendra (he/she will learn)
nous apprendrons (we will learn)
vous apprendrez (you will learn)
ils/elles apprendront (they will learn)

Objects

Direct Object Pronouns

Direct object pronouns replace nouns in a sentence. Since nouns are either masculine or feminine in French, the direct object *it* can be expressed in either masculine or feminine form. When the item you are talking about is masculine, you use the direct object pronoun *le*. If the object is feminine, you use *la*. When the direct object appears in front of a verb starting with a vowel, you always use the *l',* no matter the gender.

me	me
te	you
le/l'	it (m)
la/l'	it (f)
nous	us
vous	you (form/pl)
les	them

Indirect Object Pronouns

An indirect object names the person or object to whom the action is being performed. It answers the question *to or for whom?* There are six object pronouns in French:

me	to/for me
te	to/for you
lui	to/for him/her/it

nous	to/for us
vous	to/for you (form/pl)
leur	to/for them

Note: In French, direct and indirect object pronouns are always placed before the conjugated verb. Example: *Elle lui donne un cadeau.* (She gives a present to him).

Double Object Pronouns

Sometimes both direct and indirect object pronouns are used in the same sentence. This is called double object pronouns. There is a fixed order for double object pronouns. Some indirect object pronouns (*me, te, se, nous, vous*) come before the direct object pronoun and others (*lui, leur*) come after. Here are some examples.

Je le lui donne. (I give it to him.)
Le serveur la leur sert. (The waiter serves it to them.)
Jean me l'achète. (Jean buys it for me.)
Ils nous l'ont envoyé. (They sent it to us.)

AUDIO TRANSCRIPT

CD 1
Track 1

Hi! How are you (fam)? *Salut! Ça va?* ▪ Hello. How are you (form/pl)? *Bonjour. Comment allez-vous?* ▪ Here is *Voici* ▪ There is *Voilà* ▪ I'm happy (m) *Je suis content* ▪ I'm happy (f) *Je suis contente* ▪ I'm sad *Je suis triste* ▪ I'm fine *Je vais bien* ▪ It's far *C'est loin* ▪ It's near *C'est près* ▪ It's here *C'est ici* ▪ It's there *C'est là* ▪ It's better *C'est mieux* ▪ It's worse *C'est pire* ▪ He is at home *Il est chez lui* ▪ She is at home *Elle est chez elle* ▪ It's in the city *C'est en ville* ▪ It's in the country *C'est à la campagne* ▪ It's in the mountains *C'est à la montagne* ▪ I'm busy *Je suis occupé(e)*

Track 2

Where is it? *Où est-ce?* ▪ It is *C'est* ▪ It isn't *Ce n'est pas* ▪ What is this? *Qu'est-ce que c'est?* ▪ What is that? *Qu'est-ce que c'est que ça?* ▪ Who is it? *Qui est-ce?* ▪ What is spoken? *Qu'est-ce qu'on parle?* ▪ What is spoken in France? *Qu'est-ce qu'on parle en France?* ▪ In France French is spoken *En France on parle français*

Track 3

How do you say? *Comment dit-on?* ▪ How do you say that in French? *Comment dit-on ça en français?* ▪ What color is it? *De quelle couleur est-ce que c'est?* ▪ It's red *C'est rouge* ▪ White *Blanc* ▪ Black *Noir* ▪ Yellow *Jaune* ▪ See you later *À bientôt* ▪ What is this? *Qu'est-ce que c'est?* ▪ It's a present *C'est un cadeau* ▪ How much does it cost? *Combien ça coût?* ▪ That's why *C'est pour ça* ▪ Right away *Tout de suite* ▪ What size is it? *Quelle taille est-ce que c'est?* ▪ I'm sorry but I don't understand *Je suis désolé(e) mais je ne comprends pas* ▪ Repeat please (form/pl) *Répétez s'il vous plaît* ▪ What size is it? *C'est quelle taille?* ▪ How far away is it? *C'est quelle distance?*

Track 4

Here it (m sing) is *Le voici* ▪ Here it (f sing) is *La voici* ▪ What kind *Quelle sorte* or *Quel genre* ▪ Who is it? *C'est qui?* ▪ What is it? *C'est quoi?* ▪ When does it start? *Ça commence quand?* ▪ Why are you (form/pl) here? *Pourquoi êtes-vous ici?* ▪ I'm here because I need the money *Je suis ici parce que j'ai besoin de l'argent*

Track 5

Whose is it? *C'est à qui?* ▪ It's mine (m sing) *C'est le mien* ▪ It's mine (f sing) *C'est la mienne* ▪ They are mine (m pl) *Ce sont les miens* ▪ They are mine (f pl) *Ce sont les miennes* ▪ Where is the cup? *Où est la tasse?* ▪ It's on the table *Elle est sur la table* ▪ Where is the book? *Où est le livre?* ▪ It is under the table *Il est sous la table* ▪ Where is the fork? *Où est la fourchette?* ▪ It isn't on the table either *Elle n'est pas sur la table non plus* ▪ It's on the floor *Elle est par terre* ▪ I have to pick it up *Je dois la*

AUDIO TRANSCRIPT

ramasser • Where is the grocery store? *Où est le supermarché?* • It's next to the bank *Il est à côté de la banque*

Track 6

The family *La famille* • My parents *Mes parents* • My children *Mes enfants* • Your (form/pl) parents *Vos parents* • Your (form/pl) children *Vos enfants* • My wife *Ma femme* • My husband *Mon mari* • My mother-in-law *Ma belle-mère* • My father-in-law *Mon beau-père* • My brother-in-law *Mon beau-frère* • My sister-in-law *Ma belle-soeur*

Track 7

I'm American (m) *Je suis américain* • I'm American (f) *Je suis américaine* • We (m) are American *Nous sommes américains* • We (f) are American *Nous sommes américaines* • It is far? *C'est loin?* • It is near? *C'est près?* • It is easy? *C'est facile?* • Is it difficult? *C'est difficile?* • Is it inexpensive? *C'est pas cher?* or *C'est bon marché?* • Is it expensive? *C'est cher?* • Is it good? *C'est bon?* • Is it bad? *C'est mauvais?* • How much is it? *C'est combien?* • How many are there? *Il y en a combien?*

Track 8

I have to *je dois* • I would like to *j'aimerais* • I can *je peux* • I want *je veux* • I like *j'aime* • I'm going to *je vais* • I need *j'ai besoin* • to talk or speak *parler* • to speak French *parler français* • to speak English *parler anglais* • to sleep *dormir* • to sleep well *bien dormir* • to sleep badly *mal dormir* • to go out *sortir* • to go out a lot *sortir beaucoup* • to go out a little *sortir un peu* • to go out with friends *sortir avec des ami(e)s* • to know (in terms of to be acquainted or familiar with) *connaître* • to know France *connaître la France* • to know the United States *connaître les Etats-Unis* • to know (in terms of to know facts) *savoir* • to know a lot *savoir beaucoup* • to know a little *savoir un peu* • to know foreign languages *savoir des langues étrangères* • to know English *savoir l'anglais* • to know French well *savoir bien le français*

Track 9

I want to speak French well *Je veux bien parler français* • I would like to speak French well *J'aimerais bien parler français* • I have to sleep well *Je dois bien dormir* • I can't sleep badly *Je ne peux pas mal dormir* • I can work a lot *Je peux travailler beaucoup* • I have to go out often *Je dois sortir souvent* • I want to eat French food *Je veux manger de la nourriture française*

Track 10

to eat a lot *manger beaucoup* • I'm hungry, I'm going to eat a lot *J'ai faim, je vais beaucoup manger* • I'm not hungry, I'm going to eat a little *Je n'ai pas faim, je vais manger un peu* • to travel *voyager* • to travel abroad *voyager à l'étranger* • I need to travel abroad *J'ai besoin de voyager à l'étranger* • to buy something *acheter quelque chose* • I need to buy something *J'ai besoin d'acheter quelque chose* • to sell something *vendre quelque chose* • I have to sell something *Je dois vendre quelque chose* • to study *étudier* • to study French *étudier le français* • I want to study French *Je veux étudier le français* • in France *en France*

Track 11

I want to study French in France *Je veux étudier le français en France* • to write a letter *écrire une lettre* • I'm going to write a letter *Je vais écrire une lettre* • I'm going to write you (form) a letter *Je vais vous écrire une lettre* • to send *envoyer* • to send an e-mail *envoyer un e-mail* • I'm going to send you (fam) an e-mail *Je vais t'envoyer un e-mail*

Track 12

You (form/pl) can *Vous pouvez* • You (form/pl) can send me an e-mail *Vous* pouvez m'envoyer un e-mail ▪ To begin or start *Commencer* ▪ To begin today *Commencer aujourd'hui* ▪ I can begin today *Je peux commencer aujourd'hui* ▪ If *Si* ▪ You (form/pl) want *vous voulez* ▪ I can begin today if you (form) want *Je peux commencer aujourd'hui si vous voulez* ▪ To finish *Finir* or *terminer* ▪ I can finish this tomorrow *Je peux finir ceci demain* or *Je peux terminer ceci demain* ▪ I would like to order now *Je voudrais commander maintenant* or *J'aimerais commander maintenant*

CD 2
Track 1

to pay *payer* ▪ to pay the bill *payer l'addition* ▪ I would like to pay the bill now please *J'aimerais payer l'addition maintenant s'il vous plaît* ▪ to go to work *aller travailler* ▪ I am going to go to work *Je vais aller travailler* ▪ I have to go to work *Je dois aller travailler* ▪ to return *rendre* ▪ to return the change *rendre la monnaie* ▪ I have to return your (form) change *Je dois rendre votre monnaie* ▪ You (form) have to return my change *Vous devez rendre ma monnaie* ▪ to return (in terms of to go back) *revenir* or *rentrer* ▪ to my house *rentrer à la maison chez moi* ▪ to your (fam) house *chez toi*

Track 2

To your (form/pl) house *Chez vous* ▪ To their (m sing) house *Chez eux* ▪ To their (f pl) house *Chez elles* ▪ To their (m pl) house *Chez eux* but to his house would be *chez lui* ▪ I have to go back to his house *Je dois rentrer chez lui* ▪ He has to come back to my house *Il doit rentrer chez moi* ▪ We have to go back to their (m pl) house *Nous devons rentrer chez eux* ▪ I need to ask a question *J'ai besoin de poser une question* ▪ To ask a question *Poser une question* ▪ I need to ask you (form or pl) a question *J'ai besoin de vous poser une question*

Track 3

to answer *Répondre* ▪ Answer (form) the telephone please *Répondez au téléphone s'il vous plaît* ▪ The phone is ringing, I have to answer it *Le téléphone sonne, je dois y répondre* ▪ To drive *Conduire* ▪ To drive a car *Conduire une voiture* ▪ To drive my car *Conduire ma voiture* ▪ To drive your (fam) car *Conduire ta voiture* ▪ May I drive your (fam) car? *Est-ce que je pourrais conduire ta voiture?* ▪ Note the polite form *je pourrais* as opposed to *je peux* which is *I can* ▪ You (form/pl) could drive my car *Vous pourriez conduire ma voiture* ▪ To say or to tell *Dire* ▪ To tell the truth *Dire la vérité* ▪ It's necessary to tell the truth *Il faut dire la vérité* ▪ Tell me (fam) the truth *Dis-moi la vérité*

Track 4

Tell me (form) the truth *Dites-moi la vérité* ▪ To tell a lie *Dire un mensonge* ▪ Don't tell (fam) lies *Ne mens pas* ▪ Don't tell (fam) any lies *Ne dis pas de mensonges* ▪ Don't tell (form) any lies *Ne dites pas de mensonges* ▪ To enter or to go in *Entrer* ▪ To go into the room *Entrer dans la pièce* ▪ To go into the bedroom *Entrer dans la chambre* ▪ To go into the house *Entrer dans la maison* ▪ I went into the house *Je suis entré(e) dans la maison* ▪ I went in to the kitchen *Je suis entré(e) dans la cuisine* ▪ To leave or to go out of *partir* ▪ To go out of *Sortir* ▪ To leave the house *Sortir de la maison* ▪ Leave the house! (formal command form) *Sortez de la maison!* ▪ I left my house *Je suis sorti(e) de ma maison*

Track 5

I'm going to speak a lot of French *Je vais beaucoup parler le français* ▪ I like to work a lot *J'aime beaucoup travailler* ▪ It is necessary to begin today *Il faut commencer aujourd'hui* ▪ I can answer your (form) question in writing *Je peux répondre à votre question à l'écrit* ▪ I need to tell the

AUDIO TRANSCRIPT

truth *J'ai besoin de dire la vérité* ▪ You (form) need to go there now *Vous devez y aller maintenant* ▪ I'm going to respond by e-mail *Je vais répondre par e-mail* ▪ I would like to study French often *J'aimerais étudier le français souvent* ▪ You (form) have to ask the boss *Vous devez demander au patron* ▪ You (form) have to ask the boss (f) *Vous devez demander à la patronne*

Track 6

Excuse me, I'd like to pay the restaurant bill now *Exusez-moi, j'aimerais payer l'addition maintenant* ▪ I want to sell something *Je veux vendre quelque chose* ▪ I'm going to see a movie today *Je vais voir un film aujourd'hui* ▪ I'd like to return home *J'aimerais rentrer chez moi* ▪ There's a store. I have to buy something *Voilà un magasin. Je dois acheter quelque chose* ▪ I'm going to go into the room now *Je vais entrer dans la pièce maintenant* ▪ I want to eat something *Je veux manger quelque chose* ▪ Do you (form/pl) want to eat something? *Est-ce que vous voulez manger quelque chose?* ▪ Do you (form/pl) want to drink something? *Est-ce que vous voulez boire quelque chose?* ▪ I want to go out often with my friends *Je veux sortir souvent avec mes amis* ▪ I need to finish this work tomorrow *J'ai* besoin de finir ce travail demain ▪ We need to finish this project today *Nous avons besoin de finir ce projet aujourd'hui* ▪ My goodness! It's late. I have to go to work now *Mon Dieu! Il est tard. Je dois aller travailler maintenant*

Track 7

I'd like to learn French *J'aimerais apprendre le français* ▪ I'd like to learn to speak French *J'aimerais apprendre à parler français* ▪ I want to do business in France *Je veux faire des affaires en France* ▪ I have to return to work *Je dois retourner travailler* ▪ I'm hungry. I want to eat a good meal *J'ai faim. Je veux manger un bon repas*

Track 8

I don't want *Je ne veux pas* ▪ I don't like *Je n'aime pas* ▪ I'm not going to *Je ne vais pas* ▪ I don't have to *Je ne dois pas* ▪ It isn't necessary to *Il ne faut pas* ▪ I wouldn't like to *Je n'aimerais pas* ▪ I can't *Je ne peux pas* ▪ I don't need *Je n'ai pas besoin*

Track 9

I'm not going to speak Spanish. I'm going to speak French *Je ne vais pas parler espagnol. Je vais parler français* ▪ I'm not going to Mexico. I'm going to France *Je ne vais pas au Mexique.* Je vais en France ▪ I don't like to work too much *Je n'aime pas trop travailler* ▪ I don't want to eat too much *Je ne veux pas trop manger* ▪ I don't want to arrive too late *Je ne veux pas arriver trop tard* ▪ I do not want to arrive too early either *Je ne veux pas arriver trop tôt non plus*

Track 10

I don't want to write a letter. I prefer to send e-mail *Je ne veux pas écrire de letters. Je préfère envoyer un e-mail* ▪ You (form/pl) don't need to lie. You (form/pl) can tell the truth *Vous n'avez pas besoin de mentir. Vous pouvez dire la vérité* ▪ I don't need to walk inside. I need to walk outside *Je n'ai pas besoin de marcher à l'intérieur. J'ai besoin de marcher dehors* ▪ We don't have to pay the bill (restaurant) now *Nous ne devons pas payer l'addition maintenant* ▪ I don't need to leave a tip. The service is included *Je n'ai pas besoin de laisser un pourboire. Le service est inclus*

Track 11

I'm not going to the movies. I'm going to watch television *Je ne vais pas au cinéma. Je vais regarder la télé* ▪ I am not going to watch a video. I am going to watch a DVD *Je ne vais pas regarder un video. Je vais regard un DVD* ▪ I am not going to listen to cassettes. I'm going to listen to CDs *Je ne vais pas écouter des cassettes. Je vais écouter des CDs* • I'm not going to spend francs. I'm going to spend euros *Je ne vais pas dépenser des francs. Je vais dépenser des euros* • You (form/pl) don't want to buy this. You (form/pl) want to buy that *Vous ne voulez pas acheter ceci. Vous voulez acheter cela* • I don't want to return home tonight. I'd like to return home tomorrow *Je ne veux pas rentrer chez moi ce soir. J'aimerais rentrer chez moi demain* • I don't have to buy clothing. I have to buy groceries *Je n'ai pas besoin d'acheter des vêtements. J'ai besoin de faire des courses* • I'm not going to eat anything *Je ne vais rien manger maintenant* • I'm not going anywhere today *Je ne vais nulle part aujourd'hui*

Track 12

We're not going anywhere today. Perhaps we can go somewhere tomorrow *Nous n'allons nulle part aujourd'hui. Nous pouvons peut-être aller quelque part demain* • I never want to go out on Sunday. I always want to go out on Saturday *Je ne veux jamais sortir le dimanche. Je veux toujours sortir le samedi* • We don't need to finish this project today. We can finish it tomorrow *Nous n'avons pas besoin de finir ce projet aujourd'hui. Nous pouvons le finir demain* • I don't want to start working right away *Je ne veux pas commencer à travailler tout de suite* • You (fam) don't want to learn Spanish. You (fam) need to learn French *Tu ne veux pas apprendre l'espagnol. Tu as besoin d'apprendre le français* • You (form/pl) don't want to do business with them (m pl) *Vous ne voulez pas faire des affaires avec eux* • I want to do business with you (pl) *Je veux faire des affaires avec vous* • I don't want to eat a big meal. I prefer a snack *Je ne veux pas manger un gros repas. Je préfère un goûter*

Track 13

I need to work on the computer *J'ai besoin de travailler à l'ordinateur* • Good afternoon *Bonjour* • My name is Nicole Dupont *Je m'appelle Nicole Dupont* • I don't want to watch television *Je ne veux pas regarder la télé* • I'm not going to talk on the phone either *Je ne vais pas parler au téléphone non plus* • I can't go out with friends because it's too late *Je ne peux pas sortir avec des amis non plus parce qu'il est trop tard* • Besides I need to work on the computer *En plus j'ai besoin de travailler à l'ordinateur* • I like to work on the computer because it's a lot of fun *J'aime travailler à l'ordinateur parce que c'est très amusant* • It isn't difficult. On the contrary it's very easy *Ce n'est pas difficile. Au contraire c'est très facile*

Track 14

Good evening *Bonsoir* • My name is Guy and I am in my house *Je m'appelle Guy et je suis chez moi* • I am sitting down on the floor in front of my TV set *Je suis assis par terre devant ma télé* • What do I want to do? *Qu'est-ce que je veux faire?* • Well I want to watch television *Et bien je veux regarder la télé* • There are several interesting programs on TV *Il y a plusieurs programmes intéressants à la télé* • There are soap operas, adventure movies, war, everything *Il y a des feuilletons, des films d'aventure, de guerre, de tout* • I'm not going to watch the news *Je ne vais pas regarder les infos* • I don't like it *Je n'aime pas ça* • I can watch cartoons *Je peux regarder des dessins animés* • I like them a lot *J'aime beaucoup ça* • Why? *Pourquoi?* • Because I'm only 12 years old. I'm very young *Parce que j'ai seulement 12 ans. Je suis très jeune* • I'm not old *Je ne suis pas vieux*

Track 15

We are not going anywhere today. Perhaps we can go somewhere tomorrow *Nous n'allons nulle part*

AUDIO TRANSCRIPT

aujourd'hui. *Nous pouvons peut-être aller quelque part demain* • I never want to go out on Sunday. I always want to go out on Saturday *Je ne veux jamais sortir le dimanche. Je veux toujours sortir le samedi* • We don't need to finish this project today. We can finish it tomorrow *Nous n'avons pas besoin de finir ce projet aujourd'hui. Nous pouvons le finir demain* • I don't want to start working right away *Je ne veux pas commencer à travailler tout de suite* • You (form) could drive my car *Vous pourriez conduire ma voiture*

Track 16

To say or to tell *Dire* • To tell the truth *Dire la vérité* • It's necessary to tell the truth *Il faut dire la vérité* • Tell (fam) me the truth *Dis-moi la vérité* • Tell (form) me the truth *Dites-moi la vérité* • To tell a lie *Dire un mensonge* • Don't tell (fam) lies *Ne mens pas* • Don't tell (fam) any lies *Ne dis pas de mensonges* • Don't tell (form) any lies *Ne dites pas de mensonges* • To enter or to go in *Entrer*

CD 3
Track 1

Could you tell me when we get to *Pourriez-vous me dire quand on arrivera* • Could you recommend to me *Pourriez-vous me recommander* • Could you tell me *Pourriez-vous me dire* • Could you repeat one more time please? *Pourriez-vous répéter encore une fois s'il vous plaît?* • I'm saying that I don't understand *Je dis que je ne comprends pas* • How many miles away is it? *C'est à combien de miles?* • How many kilometers away is it? *C'est à combien de kilomètres?*

Track 2

Is the service included? *Le service est compris?* • Could you please tell me when we get there? *Pourriez-vous me dire quand on arrivera s'il vous plaît?* • How much does it cost in euros please? *Combien ça coûte en euros s'il vous plaît?* • How do you say that in English please? *Comment dit-on ça en anglais s'il vous plaît?* • How do you say that in French please? *Comment dit-on ça en français s'il vous plaît?* • Why are you (form/pl) leaving so soon? *Pourquoi partez-vous si vite?* • Could you please tell me where the train station is? *Pourriez-vous me dire où est la gare s'il vous plaît?* • Could you please tell me where I can buy tickets? *Pourriez-vous me dire où je peux acheter des billets s'il vous plaît?* • Two bullet train tickets round trip please *Deux aller-retours en TGV s'il vous plaît* • I have some money. I'm going to pay right away *J'ai de l'argent. Je vais payer tout de suite*

Track 3

Venice is how far away from here please? *Venise est à quelle distance d'ici s'il vous plaît?* • Could you please repeat everything slowly? *Pourriez-vous tout répéter lentement s'il vous plaît?* • I'm saying that I don't understand *Je dis que je ne comprends pas* • I don't know if I want to go there or not *Je ne sais pas si je veux y aller ou pas* or *Je ne sais pas si je veux y aller ou non* • Sure *Bien sûr* • Excuse me *Excusez-moi*

Track 4

Sure I can go *Bien sûr je peux y aller* • Excuse me it's not my fault *Excusez-moi ce n'est pas de ma faute* • What kind of hotel is this? *C'est quel genre d'hôtel?* • This food costs an arm and a leg *Cette nourriture coûte les yeux de la tête* • I need help. Can you help me please? *J'ai besoin d'aide. Pourriez-vous m'aider s'il vous plaît?* • I really need to find a good cheap restaurant near here *J'ai vraiment besoin de trouver un bon restaurant pas cher près d'ici* • Can you recommend one to me please? *Pourriez-vous m'en recommander un s'il vous plaît?*

Track 5

I want some of it *J'en veux* • I don't want any of it *Je n'en veux pas* • I can't do anything about it *Je n'y peux rien faire* • I want to go there *Je veux y aller* • Go ahead (fam) *Vas-y* • Go ahead (form/pl) *Allez-y*

Track 6

that's why *c'est pour ça* • Excuse me sir. Could you tell me where the airport is please? *Excusez-moi Monsieur. Pourriez-vous me dire où est l'aéroport?* • Excuse me ma'am. Could you tell me where the bus stop is please? *Exusez-moi Madame. Pourriez-vous me dire où est l'arrêt de bus?* • Please speak louder *Parlez plus fort*

Track 7

Why *Pourquoi* • Because *Parce que* • Let's see *Voyons* • Let's see, I'm not sure if I understood or not *Voyons, je ne suis pas sûr(e) si j'ai compris ou pas* • You have to pay the bill now *Vous devez payer l'addition maintenant* • If you want you may order now *Si vous voulez vous pouvez commander maintenant*

Track 8

You can get a job here in France if you want *Vous pouvez trouver un travail en France si vous voulez* • But you have to work very hard *Mais il faut travailler très dur* • I can go there (nearby) *Je peux aller là* • I can go there (far away) *Je peux aller là-bas* • Do you like to travel often or rarely? *Vous aimez voyager souvent ou rarement?* • I would like to order later please *J'aimerais commander plus tard s'il vous plaît* • I'm not at all interested in going out today. It's raining cats and dogs *Ça ne m'intéresse pas du tout de sortir aujourd'hui. Il pleut des cordes* • Why don't we go to the beach? I love to swim *Si on allait à la plage? J'adore nager* • Do you like to talk a lot on the phone? *Vous aimez parler beaucoup au téléphone?* • Of course! I have a cell phone and I use it all the time *Bien sûr! J'ai un portable et je l'utilise tout le temps*

Track 9

Would you (fam) like to go out with us? *Voudrais-tu sortir avec nous?* • I want to play guitar and to sing a song *Je veux jouer de la guitare et chanter une chanson* • Is it a good place to eat? *Est-ce qu'on y mange bien?* • Oh one eats very well there *On y mange très bien* • Dessert *Le désert* • Do you (form/pl) have to go out tonight? *Vous devez sortir ce soir?* • Is it easy to make friends in France? *C'est facile de se faire des amis en France?* • To make an effort *Faire un effort* • So it's good to make an effort *C'est bon de faire un effort*

Track 10

I really try hard to learn French *Je fais un gros effort pour apprendre le français* • I really tried hard to learn French *J'ai vraiment fait un gros effort pour apprendre le français* • Is John a teacher? *Est-ce que John est un professeur?* • Yes. He teaches in a high school *Oui. Il enseigne dans un lycée* • Is Nicole Dubois married? *Est-ce que Nicole Dubois est mariée?* • Yes. She's been married twice and divorced once *Oui. Elle s'est mariée deux fois et a divorcé une fois*

Track 11

Is Dominique married or is he single? *Est-ce que Dominique est marié ou est-ce qu'il est célibataire?* • He's single. He doesn't want a wife right now *Il est célibataire. Il ne veux pas de femme maintenant* • Are your parents American or French? *Tes parents sont américains ou français?* • My parents are American but they were born in France *Mes parent sont américains mais ils sont nés en France*

Track 12

A bed *Un lit* • A telephone *Un téléphone* • A tree *Un arbre* • A lot of trees *Beaucoup d'arbres* • There are a lot of trees in my yard *Il y a beaucoup d'arbres*

AUDIO TRANSCRIPT

dans mon jardin • A flower Une fleur • Some flowers Des fleurs • I'm going to buy some flowers for my wife Je vais acheter des fleurs pour ma femme • A bouquet of flowers Un bouquet de fleurs

Track 13

Boyfriend Un petit ami • A girlfriend Une petite amie • John has a girlfriend. Her name is Nadine John a une petite amie. Elle s'appelle Nadine • He always gives her flowers Il lui donne toujours des fleurs • He must have fallen in love with her Il a dû tomber amoureux avec elle • Let's hope that she's in love with him also Espérons qu'elle est amoureuse de lui aussi

Track 14

Expensive cher (chère) • Cheap bon marché • It seems that il semble que • Supposedly • To be right avoir raison • To be wrong avoir tort • Usually d'habitude • At this time en ce moment • This hotel is very expensive Cet hôtel est très cher • That hotel must be very expensive Cet hôtel doit être très cher • In my opinion that hotel was very expensive A mon avis cet hôtel était très cher • This restaurant looks very inexpensive. What do you (fam) think? Ce restaurant a l'air très bon marché. Qu'en penses-tu? • You can't

always judge a book by its cover Habit ne fait pas le moine (Litterally, the monk's clothing doesn't make the monk) • Supposedly he's arriving today Soi-disant il arrive aujourd'hui • It seems that he has already arrived Il semble qu'il soit déjà arrivé • I don't think that you (form/pl) are on time Je ne pense pas que vous soyez à l'heure • You (form/pl) are right. It's true what you said Vous avez raison. C'est vrai ce que vous avez dit

CD 4
Track 1

The hand La main • A hand Une main • A box Une boîte • A suitcase Une valise • My suitcases Mes valises • May I take this bag on the plane? Puis-je prendre ce sac dans l'avion? • Where may I check my baggage please? Où puis-je enregistrer mes baggages s'il vous plaît? • Do you (form/pl) like to travel often or rarely? Vous aimez voyager souvent ou rarement? • I would like to order later please J'aimerais commander plus tard s'il vous plaît • I'm not at all interested in going out today. It's raining cats and dogs Cela ne m'intéresse pas du tout de sortir aujourd'hui. Il pleut des cordes • Why don't we go to the beach? I love to swim Si on allait à la plage? J'adore nager • How many kilometers away is it? C'est

à combien de kilomètres? • Is the service included? Le service est compris?

Track 2

Could you please tell me when we get there? Pourriez-vous me dire quand on arrivera s'il vous plaît? • How much does it cost in euros please? Combien ça coûte en euros s'il vous plaît? • How do you say that in English please? Comment dit-on ça en anglais s'il vous plaît? • How do you say that in French please? Comment dit-on ça en français s'il vous plaît? • Why are you (form/pl) leaving so soon? Pourquoi partez-vous si vite? • Could you please tell me where the train station is? Pourriez-vous me dire où est la gare s'il vous plaît? • Could you please tell me where I can buy tickets? Pourriez-vous me dire où je peux acheter des billets s'il vous plaît?

Track 3

First I get up and afterwords I have breakfast D'abord je me lève et après je prends mon petit déjeuner • Where is it located? Où ça se trouve? • It's on the right C'est à droite • It's on the left C'est à gauche • It's straight ahead C'est tout droit • I know the answer Je sais la réponse • I know the town Je connais la ville • He's rich isn't he? Il est riche

AUDIO TRANSCRIPT

n'est-ce pas? • She's poor isn't she? *Elle est pauvre n'est-ce pas?* • Poor John, his girlfriend stood him up *Pauvre Jean, sa petite amie lui a posé un lapin* • I'm sorry but I'm late *Je suis désolé(e) mais je suis en retard* • I pulled an all-nighter *J'ai passé une nuit blanche*

Track 4

One hundred one *cent un* • Eight *huit* • Eleven *onze* • Nineteen *dix-neuf* • Fifteen *quinze* • Twenty-three *vingt-trois* • Thirty-four *trente-quatre* • Forty-five *quarante-cinq* • Fifty-six *cinquante-six* • Sixty-seven *soixante-sept* • Seventy-eight *soixante-dix-huit* • Eighty-nine *quatre-vingt-neuf* • Ninety-four *quatre-vingt-quatorze* • One hundred *cent* • One hundred two *cent deux* • Two hundred fifty *deux cents cinquante* • Five hundred five *cinq cents cinq* • Seven hundred seventy-seven *sept cents soixante-dix-sept* • Nine hundred ninety-nine *neuf cent quatre-vingts-dix-neuf* • One thousand *mille* • One hundred thousand *cent mille* • One million *un million* • One hundred million *cent million* • One billion *un milliard*

Track 5

What can you do? *Que pouvez-vous faire?* • I can *Je peux* • You can (fam) *Tu peux* • He/she can *Il/elle peut* • We can *Nous pouvons* • You (pl form) can *Vous pouvez* • They (pl masc) can *Ils peuvent* • They (fem) can *Elles peuvent* • I can't *Je ne peux pas* • You (fam) can't *Tu ne peux pas* • He can't *Il ne peut pas* • She can't *Elle ne peut pas* • Let's not forget the *on* form • One can't *On ne peut pas* • We can't *Nous ne nouvons pas* • You (pl/form) can't *Vous ne pouvez pas* • They (masc) can't *Ils ne peuvent pas* • They (fem) can't *Elles ne peuvent pas*

Track 6

To speak French *Parler français* • Understand the lesson *Comprendre la leçon* • To go *Aller* • To work *Travailler* • To repeat *Répéter* • To get or obtain *Obtenir* • To learn *Apprendre* • To eat *Manger* • To pay *Payer* • To order *Commander* • To remember *Se souvenir* • To drive *Conduire* • To walk *Marcher* • To see *Voir*

Track 7

I can speak French *Je peux parler français* • I can't speak French *Je ne peux pas parler français* • Can you (form) speak English? *Pouvez-vous parler anglais?* • I can't understand the lesson *Je ne peux pas comprendre la leçon* • What can you (form) do about this? *Qu'est-ce que vous pouvez y faire?* • I can eat *Je peux manger* • I can't eat *Je ne peux pas manger*

Track 8

I couldn't eat *Je ne pouvais pas manger* • I wasn't able to eat *Je n'ai pas pu manger* • You (form/pl) can order if you want *Vous pouvez commander si vous voulez* • I can pay *Je peux payer* • I can't pay *Je ne peux pas payer* • I couldn't pay *Je ne pouvais pas payer* • I couldn't pay the bill *Je ne pouvais pas payer l'addition* • Because I didn't have enough money *Parce que je n'avais pas assez d'argent*

Track 9

Can you drive? *Pouvez-vous conduire?* • Can't you (form/pl) drive? *Vous ne pouvez pas conduire?* • I can't drive because I don't have a drivers' license *Je ne peux pas conduire parce que je n'ai pas de permis* • I will be able to go *Je pourrai aller* • I can't go *Je ne peux pas y aller* • I couldn't go *Je ne pouvais y aller* • I can remember *Je peux me souvenir* • Or *Je peux me rappeler* • Can you (form/pl) remember? *Pouvez-vous vous souvenir?* • Can you remember our trip to France together? *Pouvez-vous souvenir de notre voyage en France ensemble?* • Yes I can remember it very well *Oui je peux m'en souvenir*

AUDIO TRANSCRIPT

très bien • Yes I can remember it very well *Oui je peux m'en souvenir très bien*

Track 10

Can she go too? *Elle peut y aller aussi?* • No she can't go. She already went last week *Non elle ne peut pas y aller. Elle y est déjà y allée la semaine dernière* • Yes I can remember it very well *Oui je peux très bien m'en souvenir* • What kind *Quel genre* • What kind of car do you drive? *Quel genre de voiture vous conduisez?* • I drive a Toyota *Je conduis une Toyota* • I drive a Renault *Je conduis une Renault* • What kind of house do you have? *Quel genre de maison vous avez?* • I have a two-story house *J'ai une maison à deux étages* • With three bedrooms *Avec trois chambres* • And two bathrooms *Et deux salles de bain* • What kind of food is this? *Quel genre de nourriture est-ce que c'est?* • It's French food *C'est de la nourriture française* • What kind of movie are they showing? *Quel genre de film est-ce qu'ils passent?* • They're showing a romantic film *Ils passent un film romantique*

Track 11

Why *Pourquoi* • Because *Parce que* • Why are you studying French? *Pourquoi étudiez-vous le français?* • I'm studying it because I like it *Je l'étudie parce que ça me plaît* • Why are you (form) going to the store? *Pourquoi allez-vous au magasin?* • I'm going to the store because I need to buy something *Je vais au magasin parce que j'ai besoin d'acheter quelque chose* • Why don't we go now? *Pourquoi n'y allons-nous pas maintenant?* • Because I'm afraid *Parce que j'ai peur* • Why do you (fam) read a lot of books? *Pourquoi lis-tu beaucoup de livres?* • I read them because they are interesting *Je les lis parce qu'ils sont intéressants* • Why do you (form) work? *Pourquoi travaillez-vous?* • I work because I need money *Je travaille parce que j'ai besoin d'argent* • Why do you speak English? *Pourquoi parlez-vous anglais?* • I speak English because I'm American *Je parle anglais parce que je suis américain* • I am American (fem) *Je suis americaine*

Track 12

Why are you traveling this week? *Pourquoi voyagez-vous cette semaine?* • Because I'm on vacation *Parce que je suis en vacances* • Why are you (form/pl) going to the party? *Pourquoi allez-vous à la fête?* • Because we have an invitation *Parce que nous avons une invitation* • Why are you going to the library? *Pourquoi allez-vous à la bibliothèque?* • I'm going because I like to read *J'y vais parce que j'aime lire* • Why are you (form/pl) going to the restaurant? *Pourquoi allez-vous au restaurant?* • I'm going there because I'm hungry *J'y vais parce que j'ai faim*

Track 13

What is it? *Qu'est-ce que c'est?* • I hear a noise. What is it? *J'entends un bruit. Qu'est-ce que c'est?* • I heard a noise. What was it? *J'ai entendu un bruit. Qu'est-ce que c'était?* • Someone's knocking at the door. Who is it? *On toque à la porte. Qui est-ce?* • The telephone is ringing. Who is it? *Le téléphone sonne. Qui est-ce?* • Someone knocked on the door. Who was it? *On a toqué à la porte. Qui était-ce?* • The telephone rang. Who was it? *Le téléphone a sonné. Qui était-ce?* • I'm not familiar with this food. What is it? *Je ne connais pas cette nourriture. Qu'est-ce que c'est?* • A man is walking in the street. Who is it? *Un homme marche dans la rue. Qui est-ce?* • A man was walking in the street. Who was it? *Un homme marchait dans la rue. Qui était-ce?* • Someone's ringing the doorbell. Who is it? *On sonne à la porte. Qui est-ce?* • Someone was ringing the doorbell. Who was it? *On*

AUDIO TRANSCRIPT

sonnait à la porte. Qui était-ce? ▪ There is something in the glass. What is it? *Il y a quelque chose dans le verre. Qu'est-ce que c'est?* ▪ There was something in the glass. What was it? *Il y avait quelque chose dans le verre. Qu'est-ce que c'était?*

CD 5
Track 1

I went to the gas station because I wanted to get gasoline *Je suis allé(e) à la staion de service parce que je voulais de l'essence* ▪ I went to the gas station because my car broke down *Je suis allé(e) à la station de service parce que ma voiture est tombée en panne* ▪ I need an oil change please *J'ai besoin d'un vidange s'il vous plaît* ▪ Please check the tires *Révisez les pneus s'il vous plaît* ▪ Oh darn! I have a flat tire *Ô zut! J'ai un pneu crevé*

Track 2

This is a very noisy hotel. I didn't sleep a wink all night *Cet hôtel est très bruyant. Je n'ai pas fermé l'oeil de toute la nuit* ▪ Robert glanced at his girlfriend and smiled *Robert a jeté un coup d'oeil à sa petite amie et il a sourri* ▪ His girlfriend did not come to his house. She stood him up *Sa petite amie n'est pas venue chez lui. Elle lui a posé un lapin* ▪ I always answer my telephone every time it rings *Je réponds toujours à mon téléphone chaque fois qu'il sonne*

Track 3

Sorry but I'm running late *Je suis désolé(e) mais je suis en retard* ▪ The alarm just rang and I just woke up *Le réveil vient de sonner et je viens de me réveiller* ▪ What time is it? *Quelle heure est-il?* ▪ My goodness! *Mon Dieu!* ▪ It's already 7 in the morning and I have to drive an hour and take the train an hour to get to work *Il est déjà sept heures du matin et je dois conduire une heure et prendre le train une heure pour aller au travail* ▪ What can I do? *Qu'est-ce que je peux faire?* ▪ Where is the telephone? *Où est le téléphone?* ▪ I have to call and say that I'm sorry but I'm late *Je dois appeler pour dire que je suis désolé(e) mais je suis en retard*

Track 4

What just rang? *Qu'est-ce qui vient de sonner?* ▪ The alarm just rang *Le réveil vient de sonner* ▪ What time is it? *Quelle heure est-il?* ▪ It is already seven o'clock *Il est déjà sept heures* ▪ How long does she have to drive? *Pendant combien de temps est-ce qu'elle doit conduire?* ▪ What does she have to do now? *Qu'est-ce qu'elle doit faire maintenant?* ▪ She has to call on the phone *Elle doit donner un coup de téléphone*

Track 5

It's in the suitcase *C'est dans la valise* ▪ It's 5:30 more or less *Il est cinq heures et demie plus ou moins* ▪ I'm going too *J'y vais aussi* ▪ I'm not going either *Je n'y vais pas non plus* ▪ My goodness I'm late *Mon Dieu je suis en retard* ▪ It's on the corner *C'est au coin* ▪ It isn't near. It's far *Ce n'est pas près. C'est loin* ▪ How many streets away is it? *C'est à combien de rues d'ici?* ▪ Excuse me. Can you tell me? *Excusez-moi. Pouvez-vous me dire?* ▪ The knife is on the floor *Le couteau est par terre* ▪ My spoon is on the floor also. It fell *Ma cuillière est aussi par terre. Elle est tombée* ▪ Waiter, could you please bring me another spoon? *Garçon, pourriez-vous m'apporter une autre cuillière s'il vous plaît?* ▪ First we eat and afterwards we pay *D'abord nous mangeons et après nous payons* ▪ I'm going to the movies tonight *Je vais au cinéma ce soir* ▪ I'm sorry but I don't understand *Je suis désolé(e) mais je ne comprends pas* ▪ Repeat everything slowly please *Répétez tout lentement s'il vous plaît*

Track 6

I wanted to talk on the phone but I wasn't able *Je voulais parler au téléphone mais je n'ai pas pu* ▪ A storm *Un orage* ▪ I wanted to sleep

AUDIO TRANSCRIPT

last night but I wasn't able *Je voulais dormir hier soir mais je n'ai pas pu* • There was a storm *Il y avait un orage* • I was going to go out with friends *J'allais sortir avec des amis* • But they had to work *Mais ils devaient travailler* • I had to go shopping but I ran out of money *Je devais aller faire les courses mais je n'avais plus d'argent*

Track 7

I would like to go back to France but the euro is very high against the dollar *J'aimerais retourner en France mais l'euro est très fort par rapport au dollar* • I went there last year and I loved it *J'y suis allé(e) l'année dernière est j'ai adoré* • I need to get a good French dictionary as soon as possible *J'ai besoin d'avoir un bon dictionnaire français dès que possible* • I wanted to begin working right away *Je voulais commencer à travailler tout de suite* • I thought that you wanted to eat later. Are you hungry yet? *Je pensais que tu voulais manger plus tard. Tu as faim maintenant?* • I wanted to cash this check but they wouldn't let me *Je voulais toucher ce chèque mais ils ne m'ont pas laissé*

Track 8

I had to ask for directions. I got lost *J'ai dû demander mon chemin. Je m'étais perdu(e)* • I had to begin right away. That's why I came early *Je devais commencer tout de suite. C'est pour ça que je suis venu(e) tôt* • It was necessary to pay at the cash register *Il fallait payer à la caisse* • I am going to cash this traveler's check *Je vais encaisser un travelers chèque* • I would like to buy a souvenir *J'aimerais acheter un souvenir* • I would like to go downtown and go shopping *J'aimerais aller au centre-ville ville et faire des courses* • I have to buy everything that I want *Je dois acheter tout ce que je veux*

Track 9

I'm going to want *Je vais vouloir* • I'm going to like *Je vais aimer* • I'm going to *Je vais* • I'm going to have to *Je vais devoir* • It'll be necessary to *Il faudra* • I'm going to be able to *Je vais pouvoir* • I'm going to need *Je vais avoir besoin* • I'm going to want to travel more often *Je vais vouloir voyager plus souvent* • I'm going to want to win always *Je vais vouloir toujours gagner* • I'm going to like to visit different countries *Je vais aimer visiter des pays différents*

Track 10

I'm sick *Je suis malade* • I'm not sick, I'm well *Je ne suis pas malade, je vais bien* • How is your family? *Comment va votre famille?* • Everyone is fine, thank you *Tout le monde va bien, merci* • Who is talking to you? *Qui vous parle?* • Who was talking to you? *Qui vous parlait?* • I wasn't speaking with anyone *Je ne parlais à personne*

Track 11

Me too *Moi aussi* • You (form/pl) too *Vous aussi* • You (fam) too *Vous aussi* • Neither *Non plus* • Me neither *Moi non plus* • You (form/pl) neither *Vous non plus* • You (fam) neither *Toi non plus* • First *D'abord* • Afterwards *Après*

Track 12

Handsome *Beau* • Beautiful *Belle* • It's all the same to me *Ça m'est égale* • Pardon *Pardon* • Other *Autre* • Fiancé *Fiancé(e)* • At the beginning *Au début* • Really *Vraiment* • At the end *À la fin* • While or during *Pendant* • Friend *Ami(e)* • Buddy *Copain* • Female buddy *Copine* • A little *Un peu*

Track 13

I don't care about the price. It's all the same to me *Je m'en fiche du prix. Ça m'est égale* • Excuse me, where is the classroom please? *Excusez-moi, où est la salle de classe s'il vous plaît?* • I

AUDIO TRANSCRIPT

usually listen to the radio while I study *En générale j'écoute la radio pendant que j'étudie* • I don't want this job. I want another one *Je ne veux pas ce travail. J'en veux un autre* • My friend does not study English. She studies French *Mon amie n'étudie pas l'anglais. Elle étudie le français* • I speak a lot of French and a little Italian *Je parle beaucoup de français et un peu d'italian* • Jacques has a fiancé. He is going to get married in the spring *Jacques a une fiancée. Il va se marier en printemps* • Are you (form/pl) really angry or are you just joking? *Êtes-vous vraiment en colère ou est-ce que vous plaisantez?*

CD 6
Track 1

What do you do while you're studying? *Que faites-vous pendant que vous étudiez?* • Do you speak French well or badly? *Vous parlez bien français ou mal?* • Do you have a beautiful house? *Avez-vous une belle maison?* • Did you (form/pl) like the movie at the end? *Vous avez aimé le film à la fin?* • Would you like another French book? *Aimeriez-vous un autre livre français?*

Track 2

To speak *Parler* • To understand *Comprendre* • To need *Avoir besoin* • To be well *Aller bien* • One speaks *On parle* • To have *Avoir* • To be able *Pouvoir* • To call *Appeler* • To be sick or ill *Être malade* • Maybe *Peut-être*

Track 3

I'm calling your friend *J'appelle votre ami* • He needs money right away. He's broke *Il a besoin d'argent tout de suite. Il est fauché* • My friend is sick. I hope he gets better soon *Mon ami est malade. J'espère qu'il ira mieux bientôt* • How are your parents doing? They're doing fine thank you *Comment vont vos parents? Ils vont bien merci* • In France French is spoken *En France on parle français* • Maybe I'll go to Mexico next year but this year I'm going to France *Je vais peut-être aller au Méxique l'année prochaine mais cette année je vais en France*

Track 4

Do you understand French well? *Vous comprenez bien le français?* • What is spoken in France? *Que parle-t-on en France?* • I hope that you (form/pl) are doing fine today *J'espère que vous allez bien aujourd'hui* • Could you please tell me which languages you speak? *Pourriez-vous me dire quelles langues vous parlez s'il vous plaît?* • To know facts or subjects *Savoir* • To be acquainted with people places or things *Connaître* • I know the answer *Je sais la réponse* • I know the restaurant, in other words I'm familiar with the restaurant *Je connais le restaurant*

Track 5

I knew the answer *Je savais la réponse* • I was familiar with or I was acquainted with the restaurant *Je connaissais le restaurant* • Do you (form/pl) know the answer? *Savez-vous la réponse?* • Are you familiar with the restaurant? *Connaissez-vous le restaurant?* • Did you know the answer? *Saviez-vous la réponse?* • Were you acquainted with the restaurant? *Connaissiez-vous le restaurant?* • I know the address *Je sais l'adresse* • I'm familiar with Europe *Je connais l'Europe* • I know French *Je sais le français* • I know Marie *Je connais Marie* • Fortunately I knew French *Heureusement je savais le français* • Fortunately I knew Marie *Heureusement je connaissais Marie*

Track 6

I don't know Patricia's friends *Je ne connais pas les amis de Patricia* • My customers can't speak French very well but they get by *Mes clients ne peuvent*

AUDIO TRANSCRIPT

pas bien parler français mais ils se débrouillent • By any chance *À tout hasard* • Or *Par hasard* • You don't know this town by any chance do you? *Vous ne connaissez pas cette ville par hasard?* • Alfred doesn't know my address *Alfred ne sait pas mon adresse* • But he is quite familiar with the town *Mais il connaît assez bien la ville* • My family and I are quite familiar with French cuisine *Ma famille et moi connaissons assez bien la cuisine française* • Michelle is not in Spain. Oscar is not in Spain either *Michelle n'est en Espagne. Oscar n'est pas en Espagne non plus* • I'm making a lot of money. My wife is making a lot of money also *Je gagne beaucoup d'argent. Ma femme gagne aussi beaucoup d'argent* • My friends know a lot of things. I also know quite a few things *Mes amis savent beaucoup de choses. Je sais beaucoup de choses aussi* • I'm not very tall. My sister isn't very tall either *Je ne suis pas très grande. Ma soeur n'est pas très grande non plus* • My boss never arrives at work on time. I never arrive at work on time either *Mon patron n'arrive jamais au travail à l'heure. Je n'arrive jamais au travail à l'heure non plus*

Track 7

First *D'abord* • Then *Ensuite* • First I work and then I rest *D'abord je travaille et ensuite* je me repose • First I worked and then I rested *D'abord j'ai travaillé et ensuite je me suis reposé(e)* • First I'll work and then I'll rest *D'abord je travaillerai et ensuite je me reposerai* • First I have to work and then I have to rest *D'abord je dois travailler et ensuite je dois me reposer* • First I order and then I eat *D'abord je commande et ensuite je mange* • And finally I pay the bill *Et enfin je paie l'addition* • First I ordered and then I ate. And finally I paid the bill *D'abord j'ai commandé et ensuite j'ai mange. Et enfin j'ai payé l'addition* • First you open the door and then you close it *D'abord vous ouvrez la porte et ensuite vous la fermez* • First you opened the door and then you closed it *D'abord vous avez ouvert la porte et ensuite vous l'avez fermé* • First you will open the door and then you will close it *D'abord vous ouvrirez la porte et ensuite vous la fermerez*

Track 8

First they (masc pl) turn on the light and then they turn it off *D'abord ils allument la lumière et ensuite ils l'éteignent* • First they turned on the light and then they turned it off *D'abord ils ont allumé la lumière et ensuite ils l'ont éteinte* • First they will turn on the light and then they will turn it off *D'abord ils allumeront la lumière et ensuite ils l'éteindront* • First we sleep all night and then we wake up in the morning *D'abord on dort toute la nuit et ensuite on se réveille le matin* • First we slept all night and then we woke up in the morning *D'abord on a dormi toute la nuit et ensuite on s'est réveillé le matin* • First we will sleep all night and then we will wake up in the morning *D'abord on dormira toute la nuit et ensuite on se réveillera le matin*

Track 9

Then *Ensuite* • During *Pendant* • On the contrary *Au contraire* • To like a lot *Aimer beaucoup* • Several *Plusieurs* • To go shopping *Faire les courses* • The bakery *La boulangerie* • The store *Le magasin* • The cash register *La caisse* • Sidwalk *Trottoir* • At a distance *De loin* • Deep inside *Au fond* • Whoever or anyone *N'importe qui* • Soccer team *L'équipe de football* • Limit *Le comble* • Taste *Le goût* • Often *Souvent* • Earned him the name *Lui a valu le nom* • Since *Depuis* • Cashier (f) *La caissière* • Candy *Bon bon* • Behavior *Le comportement*

Track 10

It's five past one *Il est une heure cinq* • It is twenty-five past seven *Il sept heures vingt-cinq* ▪ It is twenty to six *Il est sept heures moins vingt* ▪ It is half past one *Il est une heure et demie* ▪ It is three thirty *Il est trois heures et demie* ▪ It is five o'clock on the dot *Il est cinq heures pile* ▪ It is a quarter to three *Il est trois heures moins le quart* ▪ It is six thirty *Il est six heures et demie* ▪ It is twenty-five past two *Il est deux heures vingt-cinq* ▪ It is four o'clock *Il est quatre heures*

Track 11

Day *Le jour* ▪ The week *La semaine* ▪ The month *Le mois* ▪ The year *L'année* ▪ Five days *Cinq jours* ▪ It's been five days *Ça fait cinq jours* ▪ Three weeks *Trois semaines* ▪ It's been three weeks *Ça fait trois semaines* ▪ I've been on vacation for three weeks *Ça fait trois semaines que je suis en vacances* ▪ How long has it been since we've seen each other? *Ça fait combien de temps qu'on ne s'est plus vu?*

Track 12

What day is it today? *Quel jours sommes-nous aujourd'hui?* ▪ What month is it? *Quel mois sommes-nous?* ▪ What is today's date? *Quelle est la date d'aujourd'hui?* ▪ What week is this? *Quelle semaine sommes-nous?* ▪ We will go to Quebec next year *Nous irons au Québec l'année prochaine* ▪ Do you (form/pl) also work on the computer with your friend? *Vous travaillez aussi à l'ordinateur avec votre ami(e)?* ▪ I'm not going there either *Je n'y vais pas non plus* ▪ First we'll go to the store and afterwords we'll have ice cream *D'abord nous irons au magasin et après nous mangerons de la glace* ▪ I believe Emmanuel knows my address *Je crois qu'Emmanuel sait mon adresse* ▪ But I may be mistaken *Mais il se peut que je me trompe* ▪ I know that you (form/pl) know the town *Je sais que vous connaissez la ville*

Track 13

For *Pour* ▪ During *Pendant* ▪ Dominique will be in France for a year *Dominique sera en France pendant un an* ▪ I'm doing this for you (form/pl) *Je fais ça pour vous* ▪ My train arrived late last night. That's why I'm also late *Mon train est arrivé en retard hier soir. C'est pour ça que je suis aussi en retard* ▪ I'm taking classes in order to learn French *Je suis des cours pour apprendre le français* ▪ Listen (form/pl) this present is not for me. It's for you *Ecoutez ce cadeau n'est pas pour moi. Il est pour vous* ▪ In order to speak French well it is necessary to study *Pour bien parler français il faut étudier* ▪ That is why they (masc) could not come *C'est pour ça qu'ils ne pouvaient pas venir*

Track 14

Some *Certains* ▪ Some (f) *Certaines* ▪ Others *Autres* ▪ Some speak a lot and others speak a little *Certains parlent beaucoup et d'autres parlent un peu* ▪ Some save their money and others spend it *Certains économisent leur argent et d'autres le dépensent* ▪ Some (f) come early and others come late *Certaines viennent tôt et d'autres viennent tard* ▪ Some are big and others are small *Certains sont grands et d'autres sont petits* ▪ Some (m) are tall and others are short *Certains sont grands et d'autres sont petits* ▪ Some (f) are tall and others are short *Certaines sont grandes et d'autres sont petites* ▪ Some are rich and others are poor *Certains sont riches et d'autres sont pauvres* ▪ Some are cold and others are hot *Certains ont froid et d'autres ont chaud*

Track 15

With me *Avec moi* ▪ With you (fam) *Avec toi* ▪ With him *Avec lui* ▪ With her *Avec elle* ▪ With us *Avec nous* ▪ With you (form/pl) *Avec vous* ▪ With them (masc pl) *Avec eux* ▪ With them (fem pl) *Avec elles* ▪ I'm going with you (form) *Je vais avec vous* ▪ I went with you *Je suis allé(e) avec vous* ▪ You went with me *Vous êtes allé(es) avec moi* ▪ We went

AUDIO TRANSCRIPT

Track 16

At the home of *Chez* • Are you (form/pl) coming to my house tonight? *Vous venez chez moi ce soir?* • Aren't you (form/pl) coming to my house tonight? *Vous ne venez pas chez moi ce soir?* • And in reponse to a negative question in French you do not say *oui* you say *si* • Aren't you (form/pl) coming to my house tonight? *Vous ne venez pas chez moi ce soir?* • Yes, I am coming to your house tonight *Si, je viens chez vous ce soir*

CD 7
Track 1

An animal *Un animal* • Some animals *Des animaux* • A newspaper *Un journal* • Some newspapers *Des journaux* • A horse *Un cheval* • Some horses *Des chevaux* • One hair *Un cheveu* • Some hair *Des cheveux* • A hospital *Un hôpital* • Some hospitals *Des hôpitaux*

Track 2

A bird *Un oiseau* • Some birds *Des oiseaux* • A fire *Un feu* • Some fires *Des feux* • A foreigner (m) *Un étranger* • A foreigner (f) *Une étrangère* • To a foreign country *À l'étranger* • A grocer *Un épicier* • A grocer (f) *Une épicière* • A singer *Un chanteur* • A signer (f) *Une chanteuse* • An actor *Un acteur* • An actress *Une actrice* • Who is your favorite actor (m)? *Quel est votre acteur préféré?* • Who is your favorite actress? *Quelle est votre actrice préférée?* • My favorite actor is *Mon acteur préféré est* • My favorite actress is *Mon actrice préférée est*

Track 3

It's better to arrive on time *C'est mieux d'arriver à l'heure* • What time is it? Is it time? *Quelle heure est-il? C'est l'heure?* • It's quarter to three in the afternoon *Il est trois heures moins le quart de l'après midi* • My name is…What is your (form) name? *Je m'appelle…Comment vous appelez-vous?* • Today I'm going. Yesterday I went. Tomorrow I will go *Aujourd'hui je vais. Hier je suis allé(e). Demain j'irai* • We speak English and French (on form) We are bilingual *On parle l'anglais et le français On est bilingue* • Say where are you (fam) from? *Dis d'où viens-tu?* • I like to speak and to learn French. I do it every day *J'aime parler et apprendre le français. Je le fais tous les jours* • It isn't difficult. It's easy and fun *Ce n'est pas difficile. C'est facile et amusant* • It wasn't difficult. It was easy and fun *Ce n'était pas difficile. C'était facile et amusant* • It will not be difficult. It will be easy and fun *Ce ne sera pas difficile. Ce sera facile et amusant* • Where is the train station loctated please? *Où se trouve la gare s'il vous plaît?*

Track 4

Sorry but I don't have any idea *Désolé(e) mais je n'en ai aucune idée* • Could you please tell me how much that costs? *Pourriez-vous me dire combien ça coûte s'il vous plaît?* • It's very expensive *C'est très cher* • It's too expensive *C'est trop cher* • It's very inexpensive *C'est très bon marché* • What's the weather like today? *Quel temps fait-il aujourd'hui?* • What was the weather like yesterday? *Quel temps faisait-il hier?*

Track 5

What will the weather be like tomorrow? *Quel temps fera-t-il demain?* • I don't know. I haven't seen the weather report *Je ne sais pas. Je n'ai pas vu la météo* • How is that spelled? *Comment ça s'épelle?* • How is that written? *Comment ça s'écrit?* • How many are there? *Il y en a combien?* • How many were there? *Il y en avait combien?* • How many will there be? *Il y en aura combien?* • I'm lost *Je suis perdu(e)* • I got lost

AUDIO TRANSCRIPT

Je me suis perdu(e) ▪ I got lost several times *Je me suis perdu(e) plusieurs fois* ▪ I don't want to get lost *Je ne veux pas me perdre*

Track 6

I get by in French as best I can *Je me débrouille en français aussi bien que possible* ▪ I'm making a lot of money. My wife is making a lot of money also *Je gagne beaucoup d'argent. Ma femme gagne aussi beaucoup d'argent* ▪ My friends know a lot of things. I also know quite a few things *Mes amis savent beaucoup de choses. Je sais beaucoup de choses aussi* ▪ My boss never arrives at work on time. I never arrive at work on time either *Mon patron n'arrive jamais au travail à l'heure. Je n'arrive jamais au travail à l'heure non plus*

Track 7

John studies Spanish in order to learn how to speak it *John étudie l'espagnol pour apprendre à le parler* ▪ I'm going to school in order to study foreign languages *Je vais à l'école pour étudier les langues étrangères* ▪ Marie is going to the store in order to buy groceries *Marie va au magasin pour acheter des commissions* ▪ I'm turning on my computer in order to send e-mail *J'allume mon ordinateur pour envoyer des e-mails* ▪ I'm traveling to France in order to become acquainted with lots of interesting places *Je voyage en France pour connaître beaucoup d'endroits intéressants* ▪ I'm listening to the question in order to be able to answer it *J'écoute la question pour pouvoir y répondre*

Track 8

What kind of car do you have? *Quel genre de voiture avez-vous?* ▪ What kind of car did you used to have? *Quel genre de voiture aviez-vous?* ▪ What kind of car are you going to have? *Quel genre de voiture allez-vous avoir?* ▪ I had a Ford *J'avais une Ford* ▪ Now I have a Toyota *Maintenant j'ai une Toyota* ▪ Believe me the Toyota is better than the Ford *Croyez-moi la Toyota est meilleure que la Ford* ▪ I will be in France for a year *Je serai en France pendant un an* ▪ I was in France for a year *J'étais en France pendant un an* ▪ Richard is going to the store this morning *Richard va au magasin ce matin* ▪ Richard went to the store this morning *Richard est allé au magasin ce matin*

Track 9

Richard has to go the store this morning *Richard doit aller au magasin ce matin* ▪ I work in order to earn money *Je travaille pour gagner de l'argent* ▪ Reading books pleases me *Lire des livres me plaît*

Track 10

Ninety-two *Quatre-vingt-douze* ▪ Seventy-two *Soixante-douze* ▪ Fourteen *Quatorze* ▪ Fifty-two *Cinquante-deux* ▪ Sixty-three *Soixante-trois* ▪ Seventy *Soixante-dix* ▪ Eighty-four *Quantre-vingt-quatre* ▪ Forty-one *Quarante et un* ▪ Sixty *Soixante* ▪ Twenty-eight *Vingt-huit* ▪ Thirty-one *Trente et un* ▪ Sixteen *Seize* ▪ Seventeen *Dix-sept* ▪ Twelve *Douze* ▪ Forty-one *Quarante et un* ▪ Twenty-seven *Vingt-sept* ▪ Thirty-two *Trente-deux* ▪ Fifty-nine *Cinquante-neuf*

Track 11

Pillow *Oreiller* ▪ A pillow *Un oreiller* ▪ Another pillow *Un autre oreiller* ▪ I need another pillow please *J'ai besoin d'un autre oreiller s'il vous plaît* ▪ Bathroom *Salle de bain* ▪ Toilet paper *Papier toilette* ▪ Soap *Savon* ▪ There isn't any soap in my room *Il n'ya pas de savon dans ma chambre* ▪ Hotel *Hôtel* ▪ Key *Clé* ▪ May I have my room key please *Pourrais-je avoir la clé de ma chambre s'il vous plaît?* ▪ Cashier (m) *Caissier* ▪ Cashier (f) *Caissière* ▪ Cash register *La caisse* ▪ You must cash your checks at the cash register *Vous devez encaisser votre*

AUDIO TRANSCRIPT

chèque à la caisse • At this time *En ce moment*

Track 12

Sorry but the restaurant is not open at this time *Désolé(e) mais le restaurant n'est pas ouvert en ce moment* • Supposedly restaurant is not open at this time *Soi disant le restaurant n'est pas ouvert en ce moment* • One would say that you're closing it too early *On dirait que vous le fermez trop tôt* • You (form/pl) are right *Vous avez raison* • You (form/pl) are not right *Vous n'avez pas raison* • You are wrong *Vous avez tort* • I'm never wrong. I'm always right *Je n'ai jamais tort. J'ai toujours raison* • To make a mistake *Se tromper* • I made a mistake *Je me suis trompé(e)* • In general *En générale* • Or *D'habitude* • In general I wake up early in the morning *D'habitude je me lève tôt le matin* • Usually I'm a little sleepy when I wake up *D'habitude j'ai un peu sommeil quand je me réveille*

Track 13

I speak French *Je parle français* • Yesterday I spoke French *Hier j'ai parlé français* • I used to speak French *Je parlais français* • I had spoken French *J'avais parlé français* • I would have liked to speak French *J'aurais aimé parler français* • I had wanted to speak French *J'avais voulu parler français* • I eat the food *Je mange la nourriture* • I am in the process of eating the food *Je suis en train de manger la nourriture* • I just ate the food *Je viens de manger la nourriture* • I ate the food *J'ai mangé la nourriture* • I was eating the food *Je mangeais la nourriture* • I used to eat it *Je la mangeais* • I used to eat it but I don't eat it anymore *Je la mangeais mais je ne la mange plus* • I do or I make *Je fais* • I was doing *Je faisais* • I was doing my job *Je faisais mon travail* • I did my job *J'ai fait mon travail* • I had done my job *J'avais fait mon travail*

Track 14

I would have like to do my job *J'aurais aimé faire mon travail* • I am opening the door *J'ouvre la porte* • I opened the door *J'ai ouvert la porte* • I will open the door *J'ouvrirai la porte* • I'm going to open the door *Je vais ouvrir la porte* • I'm going to leave the door open *Je vais laisser la porte ouverte* • I am locking the door *Je ferme la porte à clé* • Yesterday I locked the door *Hier j'ai formé la porte à clé* • Tomorrow I'm going to lock the door *Demain je vais fermer la porte à clé*

CD 8
Track 1

I think *Je pense* • I think therefore I am *Je pense donc je suis* • I thought *J'ai pensé* • I thought that I had locked the door *Je pensais que j'avais fermé la porte à clé* • I must have made a mistake *J'ai dû me tromper* • I guess I didn't lock the door *Je suppose que je n'ai pas fermé la porte à clé* • Please close the window *S'il vous plaît fermez la fenêtre* • I'm running on the beach *Je cours sur la plage* • I'm in the process of running on the beach *Je suis en train de courir sur la plage* • I have the habit of running on the beach *J'ai l'habitude de courir sur la page* • I'm in the habit of running on the beach in the morning *J'ai l'habitude de courir sur la plage le matin* • I just ran on the beach *Je viens de courir sur la plage* • Yesterday I ran on the beach *Hier j'ai couru sur la plage* • I really liked it *J'ai vraiment aimé ça*

Track 2

I was running on the beach when I ran into my friend Marie *Je courais sur la plage quand je suis tombé(e) sur mon amie Marie* • Right away I told her hi *Tout de suite je lui ai dit salut* • We've (on form) know eachother for a long time *On se connaît depuis longtemps* • Afterwords we ran together

Après on a couru ensemble • I find that more agreeable because I have company *Je trouve ça plus agréable parce que j'ai de la compagnie* • The sand is very white on the beaches of Cancun *Le sable est très blanc sur les plages de Cancun* • It's also very fine *Il est aussi très fin* • The water of the ocean is aqua blue *L'eau de l'océan est bleue foncée* • I love running on the beach in Cancun *J'adore courir sur la plage à Cancun* • What are you (form/pl) doing right now? *Que faites-vous maintenant?* • I'm writing a letter *J'écris une lettre* • I'm in the process of writing a letter *Je suis en train d'écrire une lettre* • I just wrote a letter *Je viens d'écrire une lettre* • I wrote a letter yesterday *J'ai écrit une lettre hier* • And I sent it by mail *Et je l'ai envoyée par courrier*

Track 3

To tell you the truth *À vrai dire* • I prefer a thousand times over e-mail *Je préfère l'e-mail mille fois plus* • Since it is so fast so easy and so inexpensive *Comme c'est si rapide si facile et si bon marché* • What did you (form/pl) do yesterday? *Qu'est-ce que vous avez fait hier?* • What did you used to do in the mornings? *Qu'est-ce que vous faisiez le matin?* • I was in the habit of reading in the morning *J'avais l'habitude de lire le matin* • In fact I read a book this morning *En fait j'ai lu un livre ce matin* • I was in the process of reading when you (form) called me on the phone *J'étais en train de lire quand vous m'avez téléphoné* • But don't worry you didn't really interrupt me *Mais ne vous inquiétez pas vous ne m'avez pas vraiment intérrompu(e)* • Frankly our conversation pleased me *Franchement notre conversation m'a plu(e)* • You can call me any time in the morning *Vous pouvez m'appeler n'importe quand le matin* • Feel free to give me a ring *N'hésitez pas à me donner un coup de fil*

Track 4

A round-trip ticket please *Un aller-retour s'il vous plaît* • What time does the train leave? *À quelle heure est-ce que le train part?* • What time does the train leave? *À quelle heure part le train?* • What time does the plane leave? *À quelle heure part l'avion?* • What time does the bus leave? *À quelle heure part le bus?* • What time does the train arrive? *À quelle heure arrive le train?* • At what platform does the train arrive? *Sur quel quai le train arrive?* • On which platform does the train leave? *De quel quai part le train?* • What time does the boat leave? *À quelle heure part le bateau?* • What time does our flight leave? *À quelle heure part notre vol?* • At what time does our flight arrive? *À quelle heure arrive notre vol?* • What floor is it located on? *À quel étage se trouve-t-il?* • Where is the airport located please? *Où se trouve l'aéroport s'il vous plaît?* • How do I get down town please? *Comment puis-je aller au centre-ville ville s'il vous plaît?* • Where is the nearest hospital please? *Où est l'hôpital le plus proche s'il vous plaît?* • Could you please tell me where a good restaurant is? *Pourriez-vous me dire où se trouve un bon restaurant s'il vous plaît?* • Excuse me. Please tell me where the American embassy is. *Excusez-moi. Pourriez-vous me dire où se trouve l'ambassade américaine s'il vous plaît?*

Track 5

I am lost. Could you please tell me where this hotel is located? *Je suis perdu(e). Pourriez-vous me dire où se trouve cet hôtel s'il vous plaît?* • Where is the shortest road to the beach please? *Où est le chemin le plus court pour la plage s'il vous plaît?* • Where is the nearest park? *Où est le parc le plus proche?* • Is there a bank near here? *Est-ce qu'il y a une banque près d'ici?* • Where is the post office please? *Où est le bureau de poste s'il vous plaît?*

AUDIO TRANSCRIPT

Track 6

I would like to order now please *J'aimerais commander maintenant s'il vous plaît* • I don't know where it is. Repeat please *Je ne sais où c'est. Répétez s'il vous plaît* • What is the room number? *Quel est le numéro de la chambre?* • Sir, my key please *Monsieur, ma clé s'il vous plaît* • Where may I leave my luggage? *Où puis-je laisser mes baggages?* • Where do the taxis pass by? *Par où passent les taxis?* • Where do the buses pass by? *Par où passent les bus?* • What will you charge from here to? *Combien vous faites payer d'ici à?* • I would like to pay now *J'aimerais payer maintenant* • Where do I pick up my luggage? *Où est-ce que je récupère mes baggages?* • Do you accept credit cards? *Vous acceptez les cartes de crédit?*

Track 7

I would like a single room *J'aimerais une chambre simple* • I would like a double room *J'aimerais une chambre double* • I would like two beds *J'aimerais deux lits* • I need extra towels, soap and shampoo please *J'ai besoin de plus de serviettes, de savon et de shampooing, s'il vous plaît* • May I have the restaurant bill please? *Puis-je avoir l'addition s'il vous plaît?* • May I have the hotel bill please? *Puis-je avoir la facture s'il vous plaît?* • There seems to be an error in the bill *Il semble avoir une erreur dans la facture* • There seems to be a mistake in the bill (restaurant) *Il semble avoir une erreur dans l'addition* • Where can I call overseas? *Où puis-je appeler l'étranger?* • How do I call abroad please? *Comment j'appelle l'étranger s'il vous plaît?*

Track 8

What did you (form/pl) do yesterday? *Qu'est-ce que vous avez fait hier?* • What did you used to do in the mornings? *Qu'est-ce que vous faisiez le matin?* • I was in the habit of reading in the morning *J'avais l'habitude de lire le matin* • In fact I read a book this morning *En fait j'ai lu un livre ce matin* • I was in the process of reading when you (form) called me on the phone *J'étais en train de lire quand vous m'avez téléphoné(e)* • But don't worry you didn't really interrupt me *Mais ne vous inquietez pas vous ne m'avez pas vraiment interrompu(e)* • Frankly our conversation pleased me *Franchement notre conversation m'a plu(e)* • You can call me any time in the morning *Vous pouvez m'appeler n'importe quand le matin* • Feel free to give me a ring *N'hésitez pas à me donner un coup de fil*

Track 9

To get/to obtain *Obtenir* • To win *Gagner* • To lose *Perdre* • To help *Aider* • To visit *Visiter* • To visit a person *Rendre visite* • To wash *Laver* • To wash one self *Se laver* • To walk *Marcher* • To take a stroll *Se promener* • To think *Penser* • To believe *Croire* • To remember *Se souvenir/se rappeler* • To forget *Oublier*

Track 10

To buy *Acheter* • To sell *Vendre* • To change *Changer* • To cash a check *Encaisser un chèque* • To look for *Chercher* • To find *Trouver* • To leave something *Laisser quelque chose* • To drop something *Laisser tomber quelque chose* • To dial *Composer* • To need *Avoir besoin* • To sign *Signer* • To sign a contract *Signer un contrat* • To open *Ouvrir* • To close *Fermer* • To leave or go out *Sortir* • To rest *Se reposer* • To get tired *Se fatiguer* • To put or to place *Mettre* • To tell a story *Raconter une histoire* • To say or to tell *Dire* • To spend time *Passer du temps* • To spend money *Dépenser de l'argent* • To send *Envoyer* • To receive *Recevoir* • To continue *Continuer* • To begin *Commencer* • To stop *Arrêter*

AUDIO TRANSCRIPT

Track 11

I wanted *Je voulais* • I wanted to get a driver's license *Je voulais obtenir un permis de conduire* • I wanted to win the game. I didn't want to lose *Je voulais gagner le match. Je ne voulais pas perdre* • I liked *J'aimais* • I used to like *J'aimais* • I used to like to help my friends *J'aimais aider mes amis* • I used to like to visit Europe *J'aimais visiter l'Europe* • I used to like to visit my uncle *J'aimais rendre visite à mon oncle* • I was going to *J'allais* • I was going to remember but then I forgot *J'allais me rappeler mais ensuite j'ai oublié* • I had to *Je devais* • I had to think quickly *Je devais penser vite* • I had to wash my clothes *Je devais laver mes vêtements* • I had to wash my hair *Je devais me laver les cheveux* • It was necessary to *Il fallait* • It was necessary to sign the contract *Il fallait signer le contrat* • So I signed it *Alors je l'ai signé* • I would have liked to *J'aurais aimé* • I would have liked to get another job *J'aurais aimé obtenir un autre travail* • I would have liked to get another job that paid more *J'aurais aimé obtenir un autre travail qui paie plus*

Track 12

I would have liked to leave a bigger tip *J'aurais aimé laisser un plus gros pourboire* • I was able *Je pouvais* • I was able to rest during my vacation *Je pouvais me reposer pendant mes vacances* • I was needing *J'avais besoin* • I was needing help *J'avais besoin d'aide* • I was needing help and you (form/pl) helped me *J'avais besoin d'aide et vous m'avez aidé(e)* • For that reason I am very grateful to you (form/pl) *Pour cette raison je vous suis très reconnaissant(e)* • I had to look for my dog *Je devais chercher mon chien* • And I had to find him quickly *Et je devais le trouver rapidement* • I was going to buy another car until I saw the price *J'allais acheter une autre voiture jusqu'à ce que j'ai vu le prix* • I wanted to find a different restaurant *Je voulais trouver un restaurant différent* • I would have liked to dial the correct number the first time *J'aurais aimé composer le bon numéro la première fois* • I wanted to choose the correct road *Je voulais choisir le bon chemin* • I managed to spend very little money in Europe *J'ai réussi à dépenser très peu d'argent en Europe* • I managed to understand her French *J'ai réussi à comprendre son français* • I'm not sure if the French were able to understand my French *Je ne suis pas sûr(e) si les Français ont réussi à comprendre mon français*